I0044990

Get Back All Your Lost Investments!

Get Back All Your Lost Investments!

How to get maximum money damages from: Bad Brokers ~ Crooked Brokerages ~ Reckless Bankers

THE FACTS ON HOW TO COLLECT MONEY FROM STOCKBROKERS, BROKERAGE FIRMS, BANKS, OR ANYONE WHO HAS CAUSED YOU FINANCIAL INJURY OR LOSS.

James J Shapiro, J.D., LLM

Copyright © 2010 by Boca Press LLC &
Copyright © by Advertising Consultants Worldwide, INC.

All rights reserved. No part of this publication may be reproduced, stored in
a retrieval system or transmitted, in any form, or by any means, electronic,
mechanical, recorded, photocopied, or otherwise, without the prior permission
of the copyright owner, except by a reviewer who may quote brief passages in
a review.

Printed in the United States of America

Second Edition, 2010
ISBN: 978-1-883527-23-5

Contents

DISCLAIMER

This publication is designed to provide general information about claims for financial loss. No lawyer should give legal advice about a specific problem or question unless he or she knows all of the facts and circumstances surrounding the case and the client. Buying or reading this book does not make you a client of the author. You become a client by making an agreement for representation with a particular lawyer. Such agreements are generally put in writing, in the form of a Retainer agreement that the lawyer will ask you to sign.

The laws in every state vary. Each case has different facts and circumstances. The author and publisher specifically disclaim any personal liability, loss, or risk incurred as a consequence of the use, either directly or indirectly, of any information in this book. The author and publisher are not engaged in rendering legal, accounting, insurance, or other professional services by publishing this book. If legal advice or other expert assistance is required, the services of a competent professional person should be sought.

SECTION ONE

INTRODUCTION

TO MY FATHER

MY father has always believed in me. He inspired me to follow in his footsteps and attend law school. Together, we formed the law firm of Shapiro and Shapiro. In March of 1986, I suggested that Shapiro & Shapiro advertise on television. Many people thought that I was too eager to develop the law practice and were against my desire to advertise. My father stood by my side. He understood that advertising would reach people who might not otherwise have access to a lawyer.

My father practiced law for more than 50 years. In those 50 years, he helped thousands of people. All of the lawyers and Judges I meet praise his compassionate heart. I am fortunate to have had such an amicable and respected person as a best friend, business partner, and most importantly, as a father.

In 2003, Sidney found out that he had cancer. He did not want to spend his final days at a hospital and moved into my house. He enjoyed his last weeks with his wife, children and grandchildren. On Halloween day in 2003, at my home, a great man went to "be with his mother" in "heaven." I am fortunate to have had so many great years with him.

A PERSONAL INTRODUCTION FROM JAMES J. SHAPIRO, ESQ.

MY name is James Shapiro. I have helped thousands of people collect millions of dollars for their legal claims. I am proud to be known as a tough, smart lawyer who gets results.

I only represent victims. I never represent corporations or insurance companies. I have one goal. That goal is to help victims collect what is fair and right.

For years, I have fought insurance companies, large corporations, and other defendants. I know that this is the only way to protect my clients' legal rights.

This book contains information about how to obtain cash and benefits if you have suffered losses due to misrepresentations by stockbrokers and brokerage firms.

For readers who need a lawyer, this book will describe how to hire a lawyer on a contingent fee basis—at no cost unless you win. For readers who are close to settling a claim, this book contains important questions to ask your lawyer before you settle.

I believe the greatest thing I can do as an attorney is to help victims obtain what is just and fair.

WHAT THIS BOOK
CAN DO FOR YOU

THIS book will answer many questions that you may have, and will tell you secrets that stockbrokers and investment firms hope you will never know:

- What to do if you have sustained financial losses due to investments.
- What is insurance company bad faith?
- What constitutes actionable misconduct by a stockbroker?
- How to win money even if:

—You consented to a risky investment

- How to select the best lawyer for your case.
- How to determine the value of your case.
- How to decide whether to go to court or settle.
- A checklist to review before you settle any case.

Stockbrokers and investment firms have investigators, expert witnesses, lawyers, and lots of money. Most individuals lack such resources—and the other side knows it. This book contains information that will help you to fight back. With this information, you can collect the cash and benefits to which you are entitled!

GET ALL OF THE FACTS on how to COLLECT MONEY from STOCKBROKERS and INVESTMENT FIRMS

SECTION TWO

STOCKBROKER MISCONDUCT

IS YOUR STOCKBROKER
ON YOUR SIDE?

STOCKBROKERS are salespeople. Stockbrokers generally work for brokerage firms, which make commissions when an investor buys or sells securities. The brokerage firm pays the stockbroker a percentage of the firm's commission on the transaction. The more transactions that a particular broker handles, the more commissions that are generated for the brokerage firm and thus for the individual broker. While brokers want investors to use their services, they may not keep track of how much profit an individual investor makes or how much loss they incur.

The goals of the brokerage firm (large commissions) and the goal of the investors (income and appreciation) have little common ground. When an investment yields a large return to the investor, the broker does not earn any additional commission. The broker's earnings are based on the volume of business that he or she generates for the brokerage firm. Therefore, the broker has a disincentive for making a sale from which the investor will reap large profits.

Where the brokerage firm offers large commissions for selling particular securities, brokers have an incentive to sell those securities to investors. But ironically, payment of a large commission to the broker lowers the chance of the investor earning a profit. For example, sales of limited partnerships can earn the broker very large commissions. The broker may be pushed by the brokerage firm to sell as much of these high commission products as possible. Often these limited partnerships are very poor investments because the investor receives a low return (yield), has no liquidity, and runs a very high risk of losing the invested money.

The unlucky investor can be subjected to much worse than inflated commissions. An unethical broker may want more than a substantial commission on the investor's account. Such a broker may try to make extra commissions by violating the rules as follows:

1. Churning-Excessively trading an account just to earn commissions.
2. Unsuitable investments—Investing money in an investment not appropriate for the investor.
3. Unauthorized trading—Buying and selling securities without the investor's permission.
4. Promises not delivered—Making promises or telling half truths so that the investor will buy an investment that he or she would otherwise not buy.

Victims of stockbrokers' misconduct can fight back. Arbitration or litigation are methods by which investors who have lost money due to improper conduct by their brokers can seek to recover their losses. Federal and State laws prohibit brokers from misrepresenting investments, omitting important information about the risks associated with particular investments and recommending securities that are unsuitable for the investor. Other actionable complaints include unauthorized trading, excessive trading and failure to carry out an investor's orders.

WHAT IS UNSUITABLITY?

UNSUITABLE investments are those that are not appropriate for the investor's financial needs and circumstances.

When an investor opens an account with a stockbroker, the stockbroker asks questions about the investor's income, net worth, liquid net worth (cash available to invest), age, investment goals and occupation. The stockbroker needs this information to determine whether an investment is suitable for the investor's financial situation. Stockbrokers have an obligation to recommend only suitable investments.

For example, an eighty year old retiree should not invest all of his or her money in one limited partnership investment involving oil and gas, for a number of reasons:

1. No investor should place all of his or her money into one investment. If the investment fails, the investor has no money left.
2. A limited partnership is an investment for the future—perhaps 20 years from now. It is not suitable for an elderly investor, who will probably not live to receive his or her money back.
3. An investment in oil and gas is often a high risk investment. Older investors generally cannot afford the risk associated with such investments.
4. An elderly investor may need income to pay bills. An oil and gas investment does not have a reliable income stream.
5.   Most oil and gas limited partnerships are not traded on an open market. If the investor needed money, the investment could not be sold to raise cash.

WHAT IS CHURNING?

CHURNING occurs when brokers encourage investors to needlessly buy and sell often, in order to generate more commissions.

Stockbrokers make money by getting a commission every time investors buy or sell securities. The more often a broker buys and sells on an investor's behalf, the more commissions the broker can earn.

It is often easy to tell that an account has been churned. If commissions paid to the broker exceed any reasonable amount of profit the investments could have made, the account has probably been oversold.

Investments are usually made for the long term. It is almost impossible for an investor to profit from frequent sales of stock, since the commissions will exceed any profit made. Only the broker comes out ahead when an account is churned.

WHY ARE SOME MUNICIPAL BONDS UNSAFE INVESTMENTS?

BROKERS have convinced many investors that municipal bonds are a safe, secure and reliable investment. Brokers may assure investors that they will receive a fair return (interest) on the investment and have the security of a state or local government to pay back the bond.

However, the broker may not tell the investor that:

1. There may be a large spread between the buy price and sell price. This price difference represents the broker's commission. The commission can be between 1/2% to 4% of the total amount invested. Most investors <u>never</u> <u>know</u> <u>the</u> <u>commission</u> received by their broker on a municipal bond purchase or sale.

   Brokers often have discretion to markup or markdown the bonds depending on what price they think the investor will pay (where the investor is buying bonds) or accept (where the investor is selling bonds). This discretionary markup or markdown can change the amount of the broker's commission, and the amount that the investor pays for the bond or receives from the bond's sale.

2. Not all bonds are safe and secure. Municipal bonds are only as safe as the government authority that issues them. High yield bonds can be risky investments.

3. If interest rates go up, the investor may be stuck with the low paying bonds. If interest rates go down, the high rate may not be locked in. The issuer of the bond can often "call" bonds and re-borrow the money at a lower rate. In such circumstances, the investor bears all of the risks of interest rate changes.

WHAT ARE WRAP ACCOUNTS?

WRAP accounts provide financial advice in exchange for a fixed annual fee. Investors are offered professional money management for a fraction of the investment normally required to get such expert advice. The investor is told that the brokerage firm can offer these services by pooling many small investors together. But such promises are frequently too good to be true.

Wrap accounts often come with large annual fees—sometimes up to 5% of the assets in the account. Yet the investor may be unaware of the hidden charges that are part of the wrap fee.

An investor who purchases a wrap account is paying one manager to manage the stocks and bonds in the portfolio, and a second manager—usually the brokerage firm—to manage the manager. Such management fees may be taken as a fee, or directly out of the assets of the fund.

Further, the wrap fee must cover a profit for the investor's own broker. By adding layer after layer of managers and brokers, the investor's "one-time" annual fee is so high that an unrealistic profit is needed to just break even.

Any trades that the investor executes may also carry fees, which are generally not included in the wrap fee. Most funds must execute their trades through the brokerage house that sends the business to them. This prevents the fund manager from obtaining the best price on a trade.

Brokers love to sell wrap accounts, because such accounts guarantee a commission on the investor's account for the whole year and require little to no work by the broker.

In summary, the broker may neglect to tell the wrap investor that:

1. The broker receives a large yearly payment just for selling a wrap investment;
2. The brokerage firm charges a large fee for picking out the "best" money manager;
3. The money manager also gets paid for overseeing your investment;

4. All trades may be required to be made through the brokerage firm
    that recommended the wrap account. No competition exists to lower
    the commissions or spreads. Even worse, since the money cannot be
    spread over many brokerage firms, the price of the investment could be
    severely hurt by the large size of the trade.

ARBITRATION

W̲HAT IS ARBITRATION?

WHEN an investor opens a new account at a brokerage firm, the investor must sign an agreement that governs the investor's rights in the event of a dispute with the firm. In most cases, the investor agrees that disputes will be resolved by arbitration rather than through a lawsuit in court.

Arbitration is an alternative to the courts to resolve disputes. The goal of arbitration is to resolve disputes quickly, inexpensively, and fairly.

The dispute is referred to one or more impartial persons who act as arbitrators. The arbitrators hear all of the evidence relating to the dispute, and then make a final and binding determination. Arbitration is private and informal.

The parties can agree in advance on certain arbitrators or can follow a procedure set up by an independent arbitration organization, such as the American Arbitration Association, to select the arbitrators.

After the arbitrators are selected, the parties must prepare for the arbitration hearing. All communications and preparations for the arbitration hearing are conducted through the arbitration organization. The arbitrators are not informed of the parties' positions until the actual hearing. Therefore, it is unlikely that evidence or arguments will be given to the arbitrators without the other party having an opportunity to contest the argument or evidence.

The parties are responsible for assembling all documents and papers needed for the hearing. As part of this preparation, the investor can request documents from the stock-broker or brokerage firm. The investor should also obtain interviews of all of the witnesses before the arbitration. Parties can subpoena documents or witnesses.

The parties should make sure arrangements are made to record the arbitration.

Each party has the right to be represented by a lawyer at the hearing. Each party can present their case to the arbitrators. In most claims, the party bringing the claim presents their side first. The legal procedures followed at arbitration hearings are similar to those used in court trials. The rules of evidence are not as strictly followed at arbitration as at trial.

Most arbitration hearings proceed in the following order:

First, there is a brief opening statement by each party. Next, the claimant tells the arbitrators the remedy sought. The claimant must explain how the remedy sought is within the arbitrators' authority. Next, the witnesses testify. Cross-examination is allowed. Finally, a closing statement is given by each party.

After both sides have presented their arguments, the arbitrators declare the hearing closed. In most cases, the arbitrators have 30 days to render a decision. A decision is called an "award" in arbitration. Most awards are binding on the parties and cannot be appealed. The awards are usually enforceable in the civil courts, if not complied with by the parties.

Most arbitrations for securities claims must be heard by an association specified in the investor's agreement with the brokerage firm. Most agreements require binding arbitration by the Financial Industry Regulatory Authority (FINRA) or the American Arbitration Association (AAA).

The main office of FINRA is 1735 K Street NW, Washington, DC 20006. Their phone number is (301) 590-6500. Their website is www.finra.org. The FINRA rules of arbitration are found on the website under "Arbitration Mediation" then "Rules". There you will find not only the rules for arbitration but mediation as well.

WHAT ARE THE COSTS OF ARBITRATION?

The cost of going to arbitration can be high, sometimes exceeding $10,000.00. Arbitration costs can include attorney fees, expert witness fees, arbitrator fees, transcript costs and fees to the arbitration association responsible for the claim. Most of these costs must be paid in advance. Most of these costs must be paid even if the investor does not recover his or her losses. The costs are as follows:

1. Claim filing fee—This fee must be paid for filing the claim with the arbitration association. For example, FINRA charges are from $50 to $1,800 depending on the size of the claim. This charge is only partially refundable and must be paid in advance. For more details see Rule 12900 in the Code of Arbitration Procedure for Customer Disputes.
2. Hearing session fees—A hearing session is any meeting between the

parties and the arbitrators. Hearing session fees will be charged for each hearing session. The Arbitration panel may assess the hearing session fees in the award, or may require the parties to pay hearing session fees during the course of the arbitration. The charges are from $50 to $1,200 depending on the size of the claim or the amount awarded.

3. Expert witness fee—Most cases require the use of an expert witness to prove investors' losses. Expert witnesses often charge between $2,000.00 and $8,000.00 depending on the complexity of the case and the time required to testify.

Securities lawyers can charge between $100.00 and $400.00 per hour. Securities cases often require extensive legal work. This could result in thousands of dollars of legal fees.

Some lawyers handle securities cases on a contingency fee basis, and will advance the costs associated with arbitration. An attorney who represents investors on a contingency fee basis will charge no fee unless money is recovered on the investor's behalf. The lawyer will take a percentage of any recovery as their fee. Naturally, a lawyer will not agree to these terms unless they are confident in the investor's case.

SHOULD YOU GO TO ARBITRATION OR SETTLE?

The brokerage firm may make an offer to settle without going to arbitration. The investor will then need to decide whether to accept the settlement offer or wait for a hearing.

The advantages of settling your claim include the following:

1. You know how much you will receive.
2. You will receive your money now rather than later.
3. You have no risk of losing and getting nothing for your claim.
4. You will not have to pay additional hearing costs and expert witness fees.
5. You will not be surprised by new information that could damage your claim.
6. You can put the matter behind you and go on with your life.
7. You will not risk the chance that the broker or brokerage firm will run

out of assets or declare bankruptcy before you win. It is useless to win if you cannot collect.

The disadvantages of settling your case include the following:

1. A settlement is final. You cannot re-open the case if new information is discovered.
2. The arbitrators could give much more money than the current settlement offer.

Many claims settle before arbitration. This is because the brokerage firms and claimants both know that arbitrators can give a large award, a small award, or no award at all. Arbitration can be expensive for both sides. A lawyer's time in court is worth thousands of dollars each day. Expert witnesses' fees can be immense. The total cost of going to arbitration, combined with the unknown outcome, often makes the decision easy.

In some cases, however, the offer made by the brokerage firm is not fair. Going to arbitration may be advantageous in these instances. A small offer means little risk if the case is submitted to arbitration.

You should consult with your lawyer and ask his or her advice on settling any claim. Law firms that handle securities claims will know the brokerage firm's tactics and will know whether a settlement offer is fair. Your lawyer will also be aware of the strengths and weaknesses of your case and will be able to advise you about the risks and benefits associated with settlement and arbitration.

YOU CAN WIN IN ARBITRATION EVEN IF YOU WERE AT FAULT FOR THE LOSS.

After you lose money in an investment, your friends and family may tell you that it was your own fault. You might think that you knew the risks of the investment and just had bad luck or made a poor investment decision.

You can make a claim against your broker and brokerage firm even if you think you knew the risks and took the risks in the following situations:

1. The broker lied to you about the real risks.
2. The investment was unsuitable for your investment situation or stated goals.
3. The broker made untrue promises or misrepresented the investment.
4. The broker "churned" the account by encouraging you to frequently buy and sell securities.
5. Too much of your investment portfolio was invested in one or two risky investments.

Investors who have sustained losses often think that they are responsible for such losses. Some investors may believe that their own greed caused the loss. Such investors should consider whether the broker created the greed by making promises of a substantial profit within a short amount of time. If the broker made unrealistic promises in order to sell the investment, the broker's conduct may be actionable, notwithstanding the investor's desire for a large, fast profit. Only a lawyer experienced in securities litigation should determine if the loss was your fault or the broker's.

IMPORTANT NAMES, ADDRESSES, AND PHONE NUMBERS

MOST arbitration hearings are with FINRA (Financial Industry Regulatory Authority). Their main offices are listed below:

FINRA (Financial Industry Regulatory Authority)
1735 K Street NW Washington, DC 20006
Telephone No.: (301) 590-6500.
Brokercheck Hotline (800) 289-9999
Their website is www.finra.org

American Arbitration Association
1633 Broadway, 10th Floor
New York, NY 10019
Telephone No.: (800) 778-7879.
Their website is www.adr.org

SEC (Securities and Exchange Commission)
100 F Street, NE
Washington, DC 20006
Telephone No.: (800) 732-0330 (Investor Information Service)
Email: help@sec.gov
Their website is www.sec.gov

SELECTING AND HIRING A LAWYER

QUALIFICATIONS

WHEN selecting your lawyer, you should consider numerous criteria. First, you should consider whether the lawyer possesses substantial expertise in the type of law involved in your case. You should take into consideration that a lawyer who specializes may be more experienced than a lawyer who practices in all areas of law. A lawyer who specializes deals with cases like yours every working day. Specialized lawyers have a greater awareness of the techniques used by their opponents to slow down and complicate the resolution of cases. Specialized lawyers' relationships with opposing counsel may also be an asset in terms of early resolution of a case by settlement, where appropriate, A lawyer who specializes may have greater trial experience than a general practitioner.

A specialized lawyer will have tried many of the different aspects of cases like yours, whereas a general practitioner may never have tried such a case. A specialized lawyer will also have a greater knowledge of different expert witnesses available to testify in regard to a particular situation, and will have a greater familiarity with the terminology critical to the case. A specialized lawyer will have a clear idea of what to expect with regard to pre-trial discovery procedures. A non-specialized lawyer may do only one or two such proceedings in an entire year, whereas a specialized lawyer handles several of such proceedings in the course of a week. The specialized lawyer will be able to anticipate what questions may be asked of the client, and therefore will better prepare the client to answer such questions. The specialized lawyer will also have a greater understanding of how to handle the extensive paper work associated with most cases, whereas a general practitioner may not have the time or resources to efficiently process such documents.

Also consider the size of the lawyer's office and what types of resources are available to the office when determining whether a particular lawyer is appropriate for your needs. A lawyer who practices alone may not have the time or financial resources required to handle a particular type of case. On the other hand, a lawyer who works as a team with other lawyers, paralegals and support staff may be able to work more productively on your case, thus offering you better results.

FEES AND EXPENSES

When you need a lawyer to help you recover for damages you have sustained due to bodily injuries, investment or business losses, or discriminatory acts, you have two choices. You can hire a lawyer by the hour. Many lawyers charge anywhere from $ 200.00 to $500.00 per hour. Such costs may be a barrier to hiring a lawyer on an hourly basis.

Your other option is to find a lawyer who works on a contingent fee basis— in other words, a lawyer who charges no legal fee until and unless you win your case. Such arrangements may be preferable to the substantial cost of retaining a lawyer on an hourly basis. In addition, you may feel more confident in a lawyer who invests time and money to fight for your case. It is unlikely that a lawyer would accept a case on a contingent fee basis if he or she does not believe in the case.

When you have your initial meeting with your lawyer, you may wish to have the fee agreement put in writing. By putting the fee arrangement in writing, both you and your lawyer prevent the chance of a disagreement or misunderstanding later in the case.

The law in most states requires the client to be responsible for all expenses the lawyer incurs to build up the case. Many lawyers charge in advance for expenses they incur in investigating and building a case, which can add up to hundreds or even thousands of dollars. These expenses include the costs of obtaining medical, financial, and employment records, private investigators, expert witnesses, filing fees, and court costs. Do not be afraid to see a lawyer because the law requires you to be responsible for these expenses. Some law firms will advance all of the money required to build up your case. The money that the lawyer has advanced to build up your case will be deducted from the settlement. Typically, such expenses are small compared to the amount that can be collected on your case.

WHAT IS A RETAINER AGREEMENT?

A retainer agreement is an agreement between the client and the lawyer. This agreement may include information on how much and when the lawyer will be paid, as well as when and who will pay for the expenses associated with investigation and litigation of the case. Most agreements in cases seeking to recover for personal or financial damages call for the lawyer to collect a fee only if the case is settled or won in court. A percentage of the amount settled for or won is paid to the lawyer. The agreement may also provide for what happens if the client decides to discharge their attorney. Further, a retainer agreement may contain the client's authorization for the law firm to investigate the claim, may permit the lawyer to stop working on the case if the lawyer discovers that there is no valid claim, and may permit the lawyer to engage co-counsel if deemed necessary.

The agreement is required by law in some states. In other states, such agreements are optional. It is good business, however, for both the lawyer and client to insist on a written agreement.

YOUR RELATIONSHIP
WITH YOUR LAWYER

YOUR relationship with your lawyer is confidential. Communications between you and your lawyer are ordinarily private and privileged. This means that your lawyer cannot reveal information that you tell him or her without your consent.

The lawyer you retain should be someone you can trust. In order to best serve you, your lawyer needs to know everything about your case, even details that are embarrassing or potentially damaging to your case.

If you do not have the utmost of faith in a lawyer's abilities, then you should not be represented by that lawyer. In the course of settling or litigating a claim, your lawyer will give you advice which your lawyer will offer with your best interests in mind. If you feel that you cannot trust your lawyer, then you will not trust your lawyer's advice. This situation can be avoided if you carefully consider your feelings when choosing your lawyer.

A lawyer is obligated to represent each and every client to the best of his or her abilities. As a professional, your lawyer should take pride in the representation that he or she offers. Further, your lawyer should be responsive to your needs regarding your case.

Your lawyer is an advocate for your claim. It is unlikely that he or she will cheat you, particularly if the lawyer represents many people with claims like yours. If such a lawyer cheated just one client, the lawyer's reputation could be ruined. A lawyer foolish enough to accept a "payoff" from the other side could lose his or her license to practice law. It is unlikely that a lawyer would risk his or her career for just one case.

While it is preferable to find a lawyer with whom you are comfortable at the start, and stay with that lawyer throughout your case, circumstances may arise under which you may elect to change attorneys. Under such circumstances, your original lawyer will be entitled to compensation for the work he or she performed on your case. This money must be paid out of the attorney's fee that your new lawyer collects when the case reaches judgment or settlement, unless you already made payment arrangements with your original lawyer.

Transferring a case from one lawyer to another can be a time-consuming process. Sometimes the lawyers will argue about what share of the fee each should receive. Your new lawyer may require time to review and understand your case. Such matters may slow down the resolution of your case.

CAN YOUR LAWYER
GIVE YOU A CASH ADVANCE?

EVEN though your lawyer may want to assist you in putting your life back together after a personal injury or a financial loss, he or she is legally forbidden from providing such help in the form of a cash advance on the proceeds of your settlement. One reason underlying this prohibition is that if a lawyer advanced you cash from your settlement, the lawyer might advise you to settle early, considering his or her own self-interest above your welfare.

The law sets strict ethical guidelines that govern relations between attorneys and their clients. If your lawyer violates these standards, he or she could be barred or suspended from practicing law. No reputable lawyer would risk his or her career for the sake of one client. Therefore, a lawyer's willingness to give you a cash advance on your settlement should alert you to the possibility that the lawyer is not serving your best interests.

HOW TO BE A GOOD CLIENT

YOU can help your lawyer in many ways:

1. Retain a lawyer experienced with your type of case.
2. Keep all scheduled appointments. If you wish to speak with the lawyer in person, call to make an appointment. Do not go to the lawyer's office without an appointment.
3. Keep detailed notes of your problems and questions so that you can review them with your lawyer.
4. Do not ask a lawyer to give a cash advance.
5. Give your lawyer a reasonable time to return your phone calls. Lawyers are often out of their offices, and thus are not always available to return phone calls immediately.
6. Be completely honest with your lawyer. Tell your lawyer everything about your claim, no matter how insignificant or embarrassing. If you lie to your lawyer or do not tell your lawyer about a potential problem with your case, your lawyer will be at a disadvantage if the problem comes up. Lawyers are used to problems and can work with you to overcome them as long as they know about the problems in advance.
7. Promptly respond to any requests your lawyer makes. For example, if your lawyer asks for copies of your medical bills, he or she has a reason for doing so, and that reason relates to your case. By quickly giving your lawyer the information he or she asks for, you can help to advance your case.
8. Tell the lawyer if you are unhappy. Lawyers need clients, and want to keep them satisfied. If you are unhappy, your lawyer needs to know why so that he or she can better serve you.
9. Remember that your lawyer wants to get the largest possible amount that is fair to compensate you. Sometimes this can take a long time.

Your lawyer will appreciate your patience while he or she is working to get you the maximum amount possible.

QUESTIONS YOUR
LAWYER WILL ASK

WHEN you first meet with your lawyer, you will be asked many questions. These are aimed at getting the information needed to investigate and prepare your claim. Your attorney can not afford to be surprised later about an important piece of information. The following is a list of common questions asked by lawyers of their clients:

1. Name.
2   Home address.
3. Phone number.
4. Age.
5. Social Security Number.
6. Marital status.
7. Spouse's name.
8. Age of spouse.
9. Children's names and ages.
10. Work address.
11. Work phone number.
12. Other phone numbers to reach you.
13. List of all persons living in household and ages and if they are dependent on you.
14. Names of any individuals, including representatives of the defendant or its insurance company, with whom you have already discussed your claim.
15. Copies of any documents that are pertinent to your claim.
16. Describe the state of your health and your financial circumstances prior to the events giving rise to your claim.
17. Provide information about your job title, duties performed, rate of pay, and hours worked prior to the incident giving rise to your claim.

18. Provide documentation of any loss of earnings that you are seeking to recover.
19. Name any witnesses to events pertinent to your claim.
20. Describe any physical problems that have arisen due to your claim.
21. Describe any collateral sources that you have received, for example, workers' compensation, unemployment compensation, no-fault benefits, disability insurance, and welfare benefits all constitute collateral sources.
22. List all expenses that you believe have been incurred as a result of your claim.
23. List all experts with whom you have consulted such as doctors, economists, accountants, etc.

CLIENT INTAKE QUESTIONAIRE

WHEN a client first meets with a lawyer certain questions need to be asked of the client. Below is a sample of some questions that might be asked about a client who lost money with a Broker.

TO: Prospective Client
FROM: Law Firm
DATE: _____

YOUR FULL NAME: _____

ADDRESS: _____

TELEPHONE NUMBERS: (home)

_____

(work)

_____

(mobile)

_____

NAME OF BROKERAGE FIRM: _____

NAME OF BROKER: _____

Please designate your account status (check all that apply):

_____ MANAGED OR DISCRETIONARY ACCOUNT
_____ SELF DIRECTED ACCOUNT
_____ IRA ACCOUNT
_____ INDIVIDUAL ACCOUNT
_____ JOINT ACCOUNT WITH SPOUSE
_____ JOINT ACCOUNT WITH OTHER
_____ TRUSTEE OF TRUST
_____ PERSONAL REPRESENTATIVE OF AN ESTATE
_____ OTHER _____
(specify)

This questionnaire is being provided to you in order to elicit information needed by us to make an appropriate determination as to the nature of your case. The information you supply in response to this questionnaire will be used, in part, to determine the viability of your case as well as in preparing any claim that may ultimately be filed. The information you provide will be maintained in confidence. Please exercise great care in completing this questionnaire. If incorrect or incomplete responses to this questionnaire are provided it will make proceeding with your case more difficult and could negatively impact any chance for recovery.

Please note that no guarantees can be made as to the ultimate outcome of your case. Additionally, if we decline to represent you, our decision may not be based on the merits of your case and should not be taken as a comment on the strength or weakness of your case. In that event, you are encouraged to consult with other attorneys who may have different opinions and you should also note that certain time limitations may continue to run which could negatively impact your case.

Please read this questionnaire carefully and answer all questions to the best of your knowledge. If a question is inapplicable, please answer "Not Applicable" or "N/A". If the answer to any question is "Zero" or "No" or "None," please so state. If you are in doubt as to any answer, please give full details. If your response to a question will not fit in the space provided, attach extra sheets and continue your answers on those sheets.

Unless a question otherwise states, answers should be given as of the date you complete this questionnaire. We will assume all information furnished by you on this questionnaire will still be valid in the future unless we hear from you to the contrary. **YOU HAVE A CONTINUING OBLIGATION TO KEEP THIS QUESTIONNAIRE CURRENT.**

Although this questionnaire may appear to be overly technical and complex, please be assured that we have attempted to structure it as simply as possible, while eliciting the required information.

1. PERSONAL INFORMATION

(a) What is your age and date of birth?

_____ years; _____ , 19_____
(name)

_____ years; _____ , 19_____
(name

(b) Are you on any disability?   _____ Yes   _____ No

If so, please describe in detail.

_____

_____

(c) Are you currently employed? _____ Yes   _____ No

Name and address of employer

_____

Job title _____ # of Years Employed
there_____

(d) Please give a brief description of your principal occupations and employment, including your position and job titles with other employers. A resume may be attached in lieu of supplying the information below.

FROM   TO   EMPLOYER   JOB   TITLE

_____

_____

_____

(e) Do you have any relatives who are stockbrokers or employed in the financial services industry (i.e., banks, brokerage firms, financial planners, accounting firms)? _____ Yes _____ No

If yes, please furnish the name of each relative and their relationship to you as well as the name of their employer and job title:

_____

_____

(f) Please list any businesses that you, or any member of your immediate family, own (include those in which you or your immediate family members have a beneficial interest in or in which you or they serve as a director, officer, or 5% or more shareholder thereof.

(g) Have you or any entity which you own(ed) ever filed another lawsuit or arbitration proceeding of any sort or ever filed a petition under federal bankruptcy law or similar state insolvency law or had such a petition filed against you or any entity you own(ed)?
_____ Yes _____ No

(h) Excluding traffic violations, have you ever been arrested in connection with a criminal proceeding, or have you ever been, or are you presently, the subject of a criminal proceeding or investigation?

_____ Yes _____ No

If so, please describe (include dates and ultimate disposition – i.e., convicted, dismissed, adjudication withheld):

_____

_____

_____

(i) Have you or any Entity in which you hold an interest ever been subject to any order, judgment, or decree (such as a consent decree) that permanently or temporarily enjoined or otherwise limited you from working in any way in the financial services industry?

_____ Yes   _____ No

If so, please describe in detail:

_____

_____

_____

_____

2. INVESTMENTS

(a) Was this your first brokerage account? _____ Yes _____ No

    (i) If no, please list all prior brokerage accounts you had previously (noting when they were opened and closed; whether they were self directed or managed accounts; whether they were individual accounts, joint accounts, trust accounts or other; amounts invested; nature of those investments (i.e., speculative, conservative); types of investments (i.e., stocks, bonds, mutual funds or combination thereof); and whether the same broker who your now complaining about was involved in those prior accounts.

Opened/ Managed/ Type of Acct. Amt Invest. Nature Same
Closed Self (indiv/joint) & Type   Broker?

_____

_____

_____

_____

(b) How much did you originally invest with the broker and brokerage firm you are now complaining about?. _____

_____

(c) What do you estimate your loss to be currently?

_____

(d) Do you have copies of all of your monthly statements from the time you opened the account? _____ Yes _____ No

If yes, please provide copies of all your monthly statements.

If you are missing some statements, please note which ones are missing (month & year):

_____

_____

Do you have copies of all of your monthly statements from your other brokerage accounts? _____ Yes _____ No

If yes, please provide copies of all your monthly statements

If you are missing some statements, please note which ones are missing (month & year):

_____

_____

_____

(e) Do you have copies of the new account documents, margin agreements or other documents that you signed when the account was opened?

_____ Yes _____No

If yes, please provide copies of same.

(f) Do you still own the investments you are complaining of?

_____ Yes _____ No

If not, when did you dispose of them? If yes, please state why you have retained them.

_____

_____

_____

_____

(g) Are you complaining about certain specific investments or trades or about the overall performance of your account?

_____ Specific Investment(s)/Trade(s)

_____ Overall Performance

(h) Are you alleging that any of the trades were unauthorized?

_____ Yes _____ No

(i) Briefly describe what it is you believe the broker and/or brokerage firm did wrong (i.e., recommended an inappropriate investment or trading strategy; made trades without permission; failed to follow instructions concerning a trade; made an excessive number of trades; failed to advise of certain risks; etc...):

_____

_____

_____

_____

(k) Have you closed the account and moved it to another brokerage firm?

       _____ Yes _____ No

If yes, please state the name of the new firm and broker. If no, why not?:

_____

_____

_____

_____

Also, if yes, please provide copies of your monthly statements and new account documents from your new brokerage firm.

(k) Did you maintain a diary, calendar or other notes regarding the date and/or substance of conversations with your broker?

       _____ Yes _____ No

If yes, please provide copies of same

3. FINANCIAL INFORMATION

The following questions should be answered both as of the date when you opened the account that is the subject of the complaint and as of today's date

	Then	Now
(a) Annual income	_____	_____
(b) Net Worth (exclusive of residence)	_____	_____
(c) Other sources of income (i.e., real estate rental income, social security, inheritance, etc...)	_____ _____ _____	_____ _____ _____
(d) Did/Do you own your own home?	_____	_____
(e) Value of residence	_____	_____
(f) Other significant assets (i.e., cars, boats, planes, art, jewelry)	_____ _____ _____ _____	_____ _____ _____ _____

Is there any other information which you believe might be helpful to us in understanding your complaint?

If yes, please describe (attach additional sheets if necessary:

_____

_____

_____

I understand that the information I am furnishing in this Questionnaire will be used by the Firm in deciding whether to represent me as well as in the preparation of a Statement of

Claim in the event I decide to retain the Firm and the Firm accepts such representation.

I further understand that until such time as I sign a retainer agreement with the Firm, the Firm has not agreed to accept representation of me in this matter although the Firm will maintain the information provided herein in confidence.

I represent and warrant that, on this date, the answers to these questions are true, correct, and complete to the best of my knowledge, information, and belief after reasonable inquiry. I understand that the answers to these questions shall be deemed continuing. If the information I have provided changes at any time and renders any of the information given herein inaccurate or incomplete, I will immediately notify The Law Firm of such changes.

_____	_____
Print Name	Print Name
_____	_____
Signature	Signature
_____	_____
Date:	Date

THANK YOU FOR TAKING THE TIME TO ANSWER THESE QUESTIONS. PLEASE MAKE A COPY.

QUESTIONS TO ASK
YOUR BROKER BEFORE
YOU MAKE ANY INVESTMENT

IT is important to learn about any investment before making a purchase. The following are typical questions that your broker should be able to answer:

1. How much of your money is actually going into the investment? How much of your initial investment goes for commissions, markups of the securities, expenses of the offer, and other related expenses?
2. How much is charged each year by the managers of the investment to manage your money?
3. How much are you charged by the owners or partners to oversee the managers each year?
4. What kind of market exists to sell your investment? Unless a large exchange exists to list and sell your investment you may suffer a large loss if you want to sell.
5. How is the return of your investment guaranteed?
6. Is this investment suitable for someone your age, with your income, with your net worth, and with your investment goals?
7. What are the risks of this type of investment?
8. What are the tax aspects of your investment?
9. What prior track record exists for the same type of investment?
10. What rate of return can you expect on your money?

HOW TO USE INFORMATION ON YOUR BROKERAGE FORM TO SUPPORT YOUR CLAIM

WHEN an investor opens a new account at a stock brokerage firm, he or she provides important information to the stock broker. This information includes details about the investor's net worth, income, cash available to invest, investment goals, property ownership, age and marital status. The answers to these questions are very important, because they inform the broker of the risks that the investor can or cannot take.

In most cases investors learn about investments from their brokers. Since brokers are professionals, it is not unusual for investors to follow their broker's advice.

If a broker sells an investment that is not suitable for an investor's financial situation, the account form is the proof that the broker knew about the investor's finances. For example, a $30,000 investment in a risky limited partnership or in options might be an acceptable risk for a young doctor earning $350,000 per year, and having a liquid net worth of more than $1,000,000. This example assumes the doctor understands the risk. However, a similar $30,000 investment for a retired widow, living on Social Security with only a $50,000 net worth is not proper.

SIPC Protection

MANY investors have been told that their investment account is protected by The Securities Investor Protection Corporation (SIPC). SIPC coverage, when available, is up to $500,000 per customer, including up to $100,000 for cash. Its main purpose is to return funds and securities to investors if the broker-dealer holding these assets can not return the assets or becomes insolvent.

The SIPC was not created to protect investors from bad investment advice. SIPC will not protect investors for the market risk in a fluctuating market. The SIPC is not a government agency.

The SIPC is a non-profit, non-government corporation, funded by member broker-dealers.

SIPC coverage usually will apply only to current SIPC members. Most brokers registered with the Securities and Exchange Commission (SEC) are SIPC members and display a sign showing their membership. You can check if a firm is a SIPC member online at the SIPC website or call the SIPC at (202) 371-8300.

EXPLOITATION OF AN ELDERLY PERSON

THE state of Florida has a statute "Fl. Stat. §825.103" that states, "Exploitation of an elderly person or disabled adult means: knowingly, by deception … obtaining or using, or endeavoring to obtain or use, an elderly person's … funds, assets, or property with the intent to temporarily or permanently deprive the elderly person … of the use, benefit, or possession of the funds, assets, or property, or to benefit someone other than the elderly person … by a person who: 1. Stands in a position of trust and confidence with the elderly person or disabled adult; or 2. Has a business relationship with the elderly person … ."

It is important for the lawyer and client to consider if the broker or brokerage firm lost investment funds to the benefit of the broker and permanently deprived clients of those funds. A lawyer needs to also determine that the elderly investor is disabled.

Your lawyer may consider the following facts:

1. Did your broker intentionally fail to disclose or explain such fees, charges and/or commissions.
2. Was the broker in a position of trust and confidence to the client.
3. Whether the client was over the age of 60 and were they therefore classified as "elderly".
4. Did the broker make false and misleading statements or omit material information like:

   a. Stating that the investments were safe and the companies were financially sound;
   b. Stating that the investments were suitable for the client and complied with their investment objectives and risk tolerance;

c. Failing to advise clients of the risk of continued losses as the market declined;

d. Failing to discuss the impact that the then current market conditions would have on these investments;

e. Failing to explain how these preferred stocks differed from corporate bonds;

f. Failing to inform the client that the companies were likely issuing preferred stock instead of bonds because they already had too much debt on their books;

g. Failing to advise the client that the call feature of long maturity preferred stocks negates the benefits of the longer maturity in a falling rate environment, so the holder does not benefit from the price increase that would occur with a non-callable fixed rate security in a falling rate environment;

h. Failing to advise Client that, with short maturity preferreds, a company with low-rated credit and a high-yield preferred will likely call in the preferred if its credit status improves, replacing it with a higher-rated bond (that is tax deductible for the issuer) but if the company's credit deteriorates, it will not call in the preferred and the price of the preferred will fall due to the deteriorated credit;

I. Failing to explain that the mutual funds invest primarily in stocks;

J. Failing to inform the client that the mutual funds exposed Claimant to the volatility of the stock market;

K. Failing to explain forthrightly the practical impact and potential risks of the course of dealing in which the broker is engaged.

L. Failing to advise the client that the specific investments recommended subjected the client to more risk than they wanted or that was appropriate for them based on their age, retirement status, income and assets;

M. Failing to advise the client that, based on their age, retirement status, income and assets, they were over concentrated in preferred stocks and/or equities;

N. Failing to advise the client that, based on their age, retirement status, income and assets, they were over concentrated in financial, real estate and other sectors that had exposure to the subprime mortgage market;

O. Failing to advise the client to rebalance the asset allocation of the accounts.

5. Did the broker make misrepresentations and omissions of material facts with the intent to temporarily or permanently deprive an elderly person of the use, benefit, or possession of the funds? Consider if the broker knew that the value of the client's account was certain to decline and that client would lose money.

6. That the Florida Statute. §772.11(1) (Civil remedy for theft or exploitation) states that, "Any person who proves by clear and convincing evidence that he or she has been injured in any fashion by reason of any violation of ... §825.103(1) has a cause of action for threefold the actual damages sustained and, in any such action ... and reasonable attorney's fees and court costs in the trial and appellate courts."

30 DAY LETTER

Your Securities Firm
MO11OO
One North Jefferson
St. Louis, MO 63103
RE: Income Loss
Mary Client vs. Bad Broker

Dear Sir:

Please be advised that we represent Mary Client, individually, as trustee of his IRA, and as Co-Trustee of the Herman Mary Client Inter Vivos Revocable Trust and the Sandra Mary Client Inter Vivos Revocable Trust, and Sandra Mary Client, his wife, as Co-Trustee of the Herman Mary Client Inter Vivos Revocable Trust and the Sandra Mary Client Inter Vivos Revocable Trust, who have sustained actual damages as a result of your actions. We will resolve this in the next thirty (30) days if you arrange payment to our clients for the actual damages sustained. However, we demand treble amount from you in the sum of $208,000.00 under Florida Statutes §772.11(1). We urge you to contact our office and resolve this in the next thirty (30) days. If you comply within thirty (30) days you shall be given a release from further liability.

Very truly yours,
Your Attorney

NEGLIGENCE

BROKERS and brokerage firms have an obligation and a duty to comply with the FINRA rules and regulations. When a broker or brokerage firm makes a mistake by failing to follow the FINRA rules or state and federal laws you should consider a claim for negligence. You should consider the following FINRA rules that your broker should follow; including, but not limited to the following:

a. FINRA Rule 2110 "A member, in the conduct of his business, shall observe high standards of commercial honor and just and equitable principles of trade."

b. FINRA Rule 2120 "No member shall effect any transaction in, or induce the purchase or sale of, any security by means of any manipulative, deceptive or other fraudulent device or contrivance."

c. FINRA Rule IM-2210-1 "Every member is responsible for determining whether any communication with the public ... complies with all applicable standards, including the requirement that the communication not be misleading. In order to meet this responsibility, member communications with the public must conform with the following guidelines. ... (1) Members must ensure that statements are not misleading within the context in which they are made. A statement made in one context may be misleading even though such a statement could be appropriate in another context. An essential test in this regard is the balanced treatment of risks and potential benefits. Member communications should be consistent with the risks of fluctuating prices and the uncertainty of dividends, rates of return and yield inherent to investments." (Emphasis added).

d. FINRA Rule 2310 "In recommending to a customer the purchase, sale or exchange of any security, a member shall have reasonable grounds for believing that the recommendation is suitable for such customer upon the basis of the facts, if any, disclosed by such customer as to his other security holding and as to his financial situation and needs."

e.   FINRA IM-2310-2(a)(1) "Implicit in all member and registered representative relationships with customers and others is the fundamental responsibility for fair dealing. Sales efforts must therefore be undertaken only on a basis that can be judged as being within the ethical standards of the Association's Rules, with particular emphasis on the requirement to deal fairly with the public. ... <u>sales efforts must be judged on the basis of whether they can be reasonably said to represent fair treatment for the persons to whom the sales efforts are directed, rather than on the argument that they result in profits to customers.</u>" (Emphasis added)).

Also consider if the broker or brokerage firm did any of the following:

Not advise the client of the risk of continued losses as the market declined;

Not discuss the impact that the then current market conditions would have on these investments;

Not explain how these preferred stocks differed from corporate bonds;

Not explain if the companies were likely issuing preferred stock instead of bonds because they already had too much debt on their books;

Not explain or to advise that the call feature of long maturity preferred stocks negates the benefits of the longer maturity in a falling rate environment, so the holder does not benefit from the price increase that would occur with a non-callable fixed rate security in a falling rate environment;

Not advise that, with short maturity preferreds, a company with low rated credit and a high yield preferred will likely call in the preferred if its credit status improves, replacing it with a higher rated bond (that is tax deductible for the issuer), but if the company's credit deteriorates, it will not call in the preferred and the price of the preferred will fall due to the deteriorated credit;

Not explain that the mutual funds invest primarily in stocks;

Not explain that the mutual funds exposed the client to the volatility of the stock market;

Not explain forthrightly the practical impact and potential risks of the course of dealing in which the broker is engaged.

Failed to otherwise perform the duties required by state, federal and self regulatory laws, rules and regulations.

Statement of Claim-
SAMPLE ONLY

BEFORE THE ARBITRATION TRIBUNAL OF
FINRA DISPUTE RESOLUTION, INC

MARY CLIENT,)	
Claimant,	)
	)
vs.	)
	)
BAD BROKER)	
Respondent.	)
_____	)

STATEMENT OF CLAIM

COMES NOW, MARY CLIENT, individually, by and through their under-signed counsel and state as their complaint against BAD BROKER INC., as follows:

FACTS COMMON TO ALL COUNTS

1. At the time the acts giving rise to the controversy occurred, Claimants resided in Boca Raton, Florida.
2. MARY CLIENT (hereinafter referred to as "Mr. CLIENT" or "Claimant" or "Claimants")
3. Respondent, BAD BROKER, is a FINRA member firm doing business in the state of Florida and is therefore subject to the jurisdiction of FINRA Dispute Resolution.
4. Non-Party bad broker 2 (hereinafter referred to as "Mr. bad broker 2") was Claimants' broker at bad broker and at all times relevant hereto was an employee of Respondent and is a person associated with a FINRA member firm.
5. This claim arises due to the manner in which Respondent, through their employee, handled the Claimants' accounts and is based upon breach of contract, misrepresentation, violation of Florida Statute §825.103, failure to supervise, and negligence.
6. In 2011, Mr. Client opened their accounts with Bad Broker. At the time they opened their accounts, Mary Client was approximately seventy-three (73) years old and retired. During his working life, he owned his own manufacturing business Mr. Mary Client came to Bad Broker after their previous broker left Brokerage Firm A. When they first spoke, Mary Client made it clear to Bad Broker that they wanted their money to be safe because at this stage in their lives, they could not recoup any losses. Pursuant to Bad Brokers recommendations, Mary Client invested over one million dollars ($1,000,000.00).
7. Mary Client set up the account as a "managed account" to be managed by investment managers. First it should be noted that the different investment advisers had different investment styles and philosophies. Thus, Bad Broker was, in effect, approving of that particular investment style or philosophy of the investment managers to Claimants by executing the trades recommended by the money managers. Additionally, despite the fact that some of the accounts were being managed by so-called "third party" advisors, it is Respondent, as Claimants' broker, who was subject to the FINRA Suitability Rule and,

therefore, it was Respondent who was ultimately responsible for the suitability of the investments in the accounts.

Bad Broker did not explain the practical impact and potential risks of the course of dealing in which the investment manager was engaged. Between 2006 and 2011 the investment manager purchased various equities Mary Client. There were purchases of approximately 1,160,028.80 worth of equities. As of November 2011, Mr. Mary Client suffered realized losses in the equities in excess of $1,402,931.46 in their managed account.

8. For example, the investment manager purchased and sold various common stock for significant realized losses including, but not limited to, the following:

1. In January 2010 and November 2010, A foods for $335,759.61; This investment was sold in November 2010 for realized losses in the approximate amount of $129,595.63;

2. In April 2010, jii Express for $37,324.80; This investment was sold in November 2010 for realized losses in the approximate amount of $22,165.29;

3. In March 2007, May 2007, September 2007, January 2008, and February 2008, Auu Intl Group for $62,379.45; This investment was sold in February, April and May 2008 for realized losses in the approximate amount of $23,320.21;

4. In September 2007, November 2007, January 2008, April 2008, and October 2008, Loan Brothers Holdings Inc. for $64,856.28; This investment was sold in June 2008 for realized losses in the approximate amount of $47,710.00;

5. In March 2007, June 2007, September 2007, January 2008, March 2008, and August 2008, Mui Lonch for $101,094.42; This investment was sold in February and September 2008 for realized losses in the approximate amount of $42,659.00;

9. In addition, the investment manager purchased and sold various mutual funds that were heavily invested in equities for significant realized losses including, but not limited to, the following:

1. In January 2005, December 2005, September 2006, and December 2006, Lii Partners Markets Equity Fund for $613,944.69; This investment was sold in November 2008 for realized losses in the approximate amount of $308,613.00;

2. In January and October 2008, Mpp Equity Fund for $473,916.17; This investment was sold in November 2008 for realized losses in the approximate amount of $204,214.98;

10. Claimants' account was over concentrated in equities. Further, the mutual funds recommended by the investment manager are heavily invested in equities. For example, the Loo Partners Emerging Markets Equity Fund Class A invests over 80% in equities. Contrary to the Claimant's stated investment objectives, Claimant is completely exposed to the volatility of the stock market. Claimant's portfolio exposed Claimant to more risk than he was made aware of by Respondent.

11. At no time did claimant or Respondent ever advise Claimants that these investments were inappropriate for them, nor did Respondent ever suggest that the Claimants should diversify their portfolio. Notwithstanding their suitability obligations to the Claimants, Respondent merely executed the trades without any discussion of the risks they were subjecting themselves to. It should be noted that bad broker is, supposedly, a "full service" brokerage firm.

12. In addition, bad broker also recommended purchases of limited partnerships for Claimants' other account that was **not** managed by any third party investment advisor. Bad broker recommended that Claimants purchase:

1. In August 2006, Amm Alternative Assets for $100,000.00; In August 2008, Claimants sold the investment for realized losses in the approximate amount of $50,030.28;

2. In May 2006, acs Private Investors for $500,000.00; In July 2008, Claimants sold the investment for realized losses in the approximate amount of $286,373.00;

These purchases totaled $600,000.00. Mr. Mary Client suffered realized losses in the approximate amount of $336,403.28 on these limited partnerships.

13. When Bad Broker recommended the purchases of the limited partnerships he advised Mr. Mary Client not to miss out on a "great opportunity" to purchase these "initial public offerings". Bad Broker strongly urged Claimants to purchase these investments and represented that the offerings were limited, that they were not open to the public, and that they were only offered to large accounts with their private bank. Claimants believed that the investments being recommended were safe and conservative and were not aware that the investments Bad Broker had recommended to them involved significantly higher risk.

14. In addition to the limited partnerships, Bad Broker recommended the purchase of several preferred stocks for Claimants other account, as follows:

1. In May 2010, Bank of Bocal Corp for $200,000.00; In September 2008, Claimants sold the investment for realized losses in the approximate amount of $9,407.67;

2. In February 2010, Crabgroup 8.125% Pfd for $211,429.00; In September 2011, Claimants sold the investment for realized losses in the approximate amount of $60,078.85;

3. In February 2009, Crabgroup 6.5% Pfd for $213,595.00; In September 2011, Claimants sold the investment for realized losses in the approximate amount of $53,023.30;

4. In February 2009, Fabulous Moie for $212,368.80; In March 2009, Claimants sold the investment for realized losses in the approximate amount of $208,038.22;

These purchases totaled $837,392.80. Mr. Mary Client suffered realized losses on the preferred stocks in their account in the approximate amount of $330,548.04.

15. When he recommended the purchases of the preferreds, Bad Broker expressly or impliedly assured Claimants that they were certain to receive their dividends and that the market value of the investments would be stable as compared to other investments. Bad Broker

representations as to the greater yield on the preferred stocks and the strength of the companies, while omitting any reference to the risks, lulled Claimants into a false sense of security and induced them into purchasing the investments.

16. Claimants suffered realized losses in excess as follows:

   a. Realized losses in the amount of $1,402,931.46; and
   b. Realized losses in the amount of $698,952.30.

   Claimants have suffered total losses accounts in excess of $2,102,608.26.

17. The investments recommended and/or purchased in Claimants' accounts were inappropriate for Claimants' accounts. Considering Claimants' age and retirement status the accounts for these elderly Claimants should have been safe and conservative since Claimants were unable to find meaningful employment that would pay them enough to replace any lost principle and income.

18. Respondent's employee's recommendations had the effect of causing Claimants' accounts to be over concentrated both as to the type of investment product and the various sectors. Respondent's employee recommended these investments with the intent to maximize Respondents' commissions rather than acting in the Claimants' best interests. For example, the limited partnerships are aggressive investment vehicles which were not appropriate for the account.

19. Additionally, when the investments were initially purchased, said purchases resulted in an unbalanced portfolio. As the market dropped and Claimants' investments declined significantly in value, the asset allocation became further unbalanced as some investments declined faster and more precipitously than others. Respondent failed to take any actions to rebalance said allocations by selling investments that were (or had become) unsuitable.

20. In addition, Respondent's employee failed to disclose that part of his bonus compensation was tied to selling certain preferred provider products. Respondents' broker received a significant portion of his compensation in the form of bonuses tied to sales of products from

preferred providers and was therefore pressured to sell such preferred
provider products at the expense of other, more suitable or better
performing products.

THE FORESEEABLE COLLAPSE

21. As far back as September 1999, the risks to these investments
    were known in the industry. For example, the New York Times on
    September 30, 1999, reported that the Fannie Mae Corporation was
    easing the credit requirements on loans that it would purchase from
    banks and other lenders. The article pointed out that, "In moving,
    even tentatively, into this new area of lending, Fannie Mae is taking
    on significantly more risk, which may not pose any difficulties during
    flush economic times. But the government-subsidized corporation may
    run into trouble in an economic downturn, prompting a government
    rescue similar to that of the savings and loan industry in the 1980's."
    (Emphasis added).

22. By early 2007, evidence of difficulties in the subprime mortgage
    market began to emerge. Between December 2006 and August 2007
    scores of mortgage companies ceased operations, either through bank-
    ruptcy or suspension of current activity. Other mortgage companies
    reported large losses and suspended their subprime mortgage lending.

23. In June 2007, Bear Stearns pledged up to $3.2 billion to bail out a
    hedge fund that made bad bets in the subprime mortgage market. A
    month later, Bear Stearns announced that two of its hedge funds that
    invested heavily in securities backed by subprime mortgages had lost
    over 90 percent of their value. Both funds declared bankruptcy on
    August 1, 2007.

24. A July 24 2007 announcement by Countrywide Financial Corp., the
    largest U.S. originator of mortgages in 2006, that subprime mortgage
    problems had spread to its portfolio of prime mortgages. Between
    August 8, 2007 and September 13, 2007 the rate on asset backed
    commercial paper increased by 84 basis points. While asset backed
    commercial paper rates had declined to early August levels by late
    September, the volume of outstanding asset backed commercial paper
    continued to decline.

25. On August 9, 2007, American International Group, one of the largest

mortgage lenders in the United States, announced that mortgage defaults were spreading beyond the subprime market.

26. On August 23, 2007, Bloomberg News reported, that U.S. commercial paper fell 4.2%, "the biggest weekly drop in at least seven years" and "[c]ommercial paper outstanding has fallen by $181.3 billion in two weeks." Many issuers turned to commercial banks, drawing on backup lines of credit.

27. In August 2007, Lehman closed its subprime lender, BNC Mortgage, eliminating 1,200 positions in 23 locations, and took an after-tax charge of $25 million and a $27 million reduction in goodwill. Lehman said that poor market conditions in the mortgage space "necessitated a substantial reduction in its resources and capacity in the subprime space". (*Kulikowski, Laura (2007-08-22). "Lehman Brothers Amputates Mortgage Arm". TheStreet.com).* Lehman continued to face an unprecedented loss due to the continuing subprime mortgage crisis. Huge losses accrued in lower-rated mortgage-backed securities throughout 2008. In the second fiscal quarter, Lehman reported losses of $2.8 billion and was forced to sell off $6 billion in assets. In the first half of 2008 alone, Lehman stock lost 73% of its value as the credit market continued to tighten and in August 2008, Lehman reported that it intended to release 6% of its work force, 1,500 people, just ahead of its third-quarter-reporting deadline in September. (Jenny Anderson; Eric Dash (2008-08-29). "Struggling Lehman Plans to Lay Off 1,500", *The New York Times*. 28 August 2008).

28. The signs were obvious, yet Respondents utterly failed to advise Claimants of the potential risks of purchasing these investments and never discussed how the above factors were certain to negatively impact Claimants' investments. Claimants were not experts in the financial industry as Respondents claimed to be. On the other hand, Respondents had the necessary expertise but either failed to do the necessary due diligence or ignored the warning signs. Claimants relied on Respondents to recommend suitable investments and advise them of the potential risks.

PROBLEMS WITH PREFERRED STOCKS

29. Preferred shares are commitments by a company to pay a set amount of interest to shareholders. Preferred shares have some characteristics that make them unique. First, just as with common stock, preferred stock-holders are behind bond holders in line for a company's assets if it runs into a financial problem. If a company fails, money is repaid to bond-holders first. The preferred stockholders are merely shareholders; no debt is owed to them. This adds default risk to preferred stock and, just as with dividends paid on common stock, a company may decide it no longer wants to pay the preferred dividend. It is this risk, particularly in light of the market conditions, that Respondents failed to adequately explain to Claimants. Instead, Respondents touted the higher yields on the preferreds in an effort to induce Claimants into purchasing them. Additionally, unlike with equity shareholders, who may benefit from the potential growth in the value of a company, but just like with those holding conventional bonds, preferred shareholders' investment return is a function of the fixed-dividend yield. The difference is that all conventional bonds have a fixed maturity date, while preferred stocks, as equity instruments, may not. Even those preferreds with callable dates will not necessarily be called.

30. A characteristic of the callable preferred stocks is that almost all call-able preferred stocks are callable at par, which means there is extremely limited upside potential if the security is purchased at par, as was the case with Claimants' purchases, and virtually none if the call date is near. Consequently, if the Claimants required liquidity it is almost certain that they would lose principle as the preferred would trade at a discount with such long term call features.

31. Even those preferreds that had call dates of five to ten years from the date of purchase were inappropriate for Claimants because the higher yields are typically a function of their credit risk. Generally, a company issues preferred stocks because its balance sheet is already loaded with a large amount of debt, and it risks a downgrade if it piles on even more, or as a way around regulatory restrictions, or because dividends are paid at the discretion of the company and in times of financial distress, preferred dividends could be deferred. Preferred stocks' call

features therefore are related not only to interest rate risk but also to the risk of changes in the company's credit rating. A company that has low-rated credit and a high-yield preferred will likely call in the preferred if its credit status improves, replacing the preferred with a higher-rated conventional corporate bond (that is tax deductible for the firm). Of course, if the company's credit deteriorates, it will not call in the preferred stock, but the price of the preferred will fall due to the deteriorated credit. This represents an asymmetric risk for the investor and provides another reason why even a relatively short-term five year call feature is inappropriate for an elderly investor. Not only were these risks not discussed with Claimants, but Respondents either failed to perform their due diligence on these companies to determine why they were issuing preferreds or simply chose to ignore the obvious.

32. While longer-term maturities with fixed yields do provide a hedge against deflationary environments, the problem with long-maturity preferred stocks is that the call feature negates the benefits of the longer maturity in a falling rate environment, so the holder does not benefit from the price increase that would occur with a non-callable fixed rate security in a falling rate environment. If the issuer is unable to call in the preferred, it is likely that it is because of a deteriorating credit, which puts the investor's principal at risk.

33. As noted above, companies that issue preferred stock rather than bonds typically do so because they already have too much debt on their books. Quite simply, preferred stock shows up as equity on a company's balance sheet while bonds show up as debt. Since interest paid on bonds is tax deductible for a company while dividends paid on preferred stock is not, the primary benefit to a company issuing preferred stock is the ability to not show more debt on the books. With the trust preferreds, the firm gets the double benefit of not having to pay tax on the dividends and not having the instrument show up as debt on its books. Companies issuing preferred stock generally have (or should have) weaker credit ratings, and distressed companies are the very ones most likely to default in deflationary environments. Consequently, the benefit of the high-yielding longer maturity (which should rise in price in a falling rate environment) is highly unlikely to

be realized by the holders of these callable instruments. None of these risks were explained to Claimants.

RESPONDENT'S WRONGDOING

7.   Respondent's employee recommended unsuitable and inappropriate investments and an inappropriate trading strategy.

   a.   The specific investments recommended subjected Claimants to more risk than they wanted or that was appropriate for them based on their age, retirement status, income and assets;

   b.   The specific investments recommended were not safe and conservative as they should have been for these Claimants' accounts;

   c.   The concentration in preferred stocks and equities was an inappropriate strategy for these Claimants based on their age, retirement status, income and assets;

   d.   The concentration in financial, real estate and other sectors that had exposure to the subprime mortgage market was an inappropriate strategy for these Claimants based on their age, retirement status, income and assets,;

   e.   The failure to rebalance the asset allocation was an inappropriate strategy for these Claimants based on their age, retirement status, income and assets;

   f.   The failure to disclose compensation arrangements that favored the sale of proprietary products.

8.   Respondent's employee had a duty to disclose all the risks involved with the above referenced investments and breached that duty by:

   a.   failing to advise Claimants of the risk of continued losses as the market declined;

   b.   failing to discuss the impact that the then-current market conditions would have on these investments;

   c.   failing to explain how these preferred stocks differed from corporate bonds;

   d.   failing to inform Claimants that the companies were likely issuing preferred stock instead of bonds because they already had too much debt on their books;

e.   failing to advise Claimants that the call feature of long-maturity preferred stocks negates the benefits of the longer maturity in a falling rate environment, so the holder does not benefit from the price increase that would occur with a non-callable fixed rate security in a falling rate environment;

f.   failing to advise Claimants that, with short maturity preferreds, a company with low-rated credit and a high-yield preferred will likely call in the preferred if its credit status improves, replacing it with a higher-rated bond (that is tax deductible for the issuer) but if the company's credit deteriorates, it will not call in the preferred and the price of the preferred will fall due to the deteriorated credit;

g.   failing to explain that the mutual funds invest primarily in stocks;

h.   failing to inform Claimant that the mutual funds exposed Claimant to the volatility of the stock market;

i.   failing to explain forthrightly the practical impact and potential risks of the course of dealing in which the broker is engaged.

9.   Respondent knew, or should have known, that the investments had significant exposure to the sub-prime market and would suffer a severe downturn as interest rates rose and adjustable sub-prime mortgages reset.

COUNT I
NEGLIGENCE

10. Claimants reallege the allegations contained in paragraphs 1 through 37.

11. Respondent had a duty to comply with the FINRA rules and regulations as well as state and federal laws, including, but not limited to, the following:

    f.   FINRA Rule 2110 ("A member, in the conduct of his business, shall observe high standards of commercial honor and just and equitable principles of trade.")

    g.   FINRA Rule 2120 ("No member shall effect any transaction in, or induce the purchase or sale of, any security by means of any manipulative, deceptive or other fraudulent device or contrivance.")

    h.   FINRA Rule IM-2210-1 ("Every member is responsible for determining whether any communication with the public ... complies with all applicable standards, including the requirement that the communication not be misleading. In order to meet this responsibility, member communications with the public must conform with the following guidelines. ... (1) Members must ensure that statements are not misleading within the context in which they are made. A statement made in one context may be misleading even though such a statement could be appropriate in another context. An essential test in this regard is the balanced treatment of risks and potential benefits. Member communications should be consistent with the risks of fluctuating prices and the uncertainty of dividends, rates of return and yield inherent to investments." (Emphasis added)).

    i.   FINRA Rule 2310 ("In recommending to a customer the purchase, sale or exchange of any security, a member shall have reasonable grounds for believing that the recommendation is suitable for such customer upon the basis of the facts, if any, disclosed by such customer as to his other security holding and as to his financial situation and needs.")

    j.   FINRA IM-2310-2(a)(1) ("Implicit in all member and registered representative relationships with customers and others is the Fundamental responsibility for fair dealing. Sales efforts must therefore be undertaken only on a basis that can be judged as being within the ethical standards of the Association's Rules, with particular emphasis on the requirement to deal fairly with the public. ... sales efforts must be judged on the basis of whether they can be reasonably said to represent fair treatment for the persons to whom the sales efforts are directed, rather than on the argument that they result in profits to customers." (Emphasis added)).

12. Respondents breached such duties by

    a. Failing to advise Claimants of the risk of continued losses as the market declined;

    b. Failing to discuss the impact that the then-current market conditions would have on these investments;

    c. Failing to explain how these preferred stocks differed from corporate bonds;

    d. Failing to inform Claimants that the companies were likely issuing preferred stock instead of bonds because they already had too much debt on their books;

    e. Failing to advise Claimants that the call feature of long-maturity preferred stocks negates the benefits of the longer maturity in a falling rate environment, so the holder does not benefit from the price increase that would occur with a non-callable fixed rate security in a falling rate environment;

    f. Failing to advise Claimants that, with short maturity preferreds, a company with low-rated credit and a high-yield preferred will likely call in the preferred if its credit status improves, replacing it with a higher-rated bond (that is tax deductible for the issuer) but if the company's credit deteriorates, it will not call in the preferred and the price of the preferred will fall due to the deteriorated credit;

    g. Failing to explain that the mutual funds invest primarily in stocks;

    h. Failing to inform Claimant that the mutual funds exposed Claimant to the volatility of the stock market;

    i. Failing to explain forthrightly the practical impact and potential risks of the course of dealing in which the broker is engaged.

j.   Failure to otherwise perform the duties required by state, federal and self regulatory laws, rules and regulations.

13. Additionally, the investment recommendations and trading strategy was unsuitable for Claimants in that:

a.   the specific investments recommended subjected Claimants to more risk than they wanted or that was appropriate for them based on their age, retirement status, income and assets;

b.   the specific investments recommended were not safe and conservative as they should have been for these Claimants' accounts;

c.   the concentration in preferred stocks and equities was an inappropriate strategy for these Claimants based on their age, retirement status, income and assets and particularly for these Claimants' IRA account;

d.   the concentration in financial, real estate and other sectors that had exposure to the subprime mortgage market was an inappropriate strategy for these Claimants based on their age, retirement status, income and assets;

e.   the failure to rebalance the asset allocation was an inappropriate strategy for these Claimants based on their age, retirement status, income and assets.

14. Furthermore, overconcentration is considered a violation of the suitability rule (*See, e.g.*, Clinton H. Holland, Jr., 52 S.E.C. 562, 566 (1995) ("The concentration of high risk and speculative securities [in the customer's] account . . . was not suitable."), aff'd 105 F.3d 665 (9th Cir. 1997)). Respondents' recommendations had the effect of over concentrating Claimants in certain types of investments (i.e., preferred stocks and closed end funds) and in certain sectors (i.e., financial and real estate) that were exposed to the subprime mortgage market.

15. Respondent's actions and breaches of their various duties proximately caused Claimants damages by causing them to incur significant losses. In addition, Respondent's employee had no exit strategy to protect Claimants from additional losses as the market declined. Respondent's employee had a duty to recommend appropriate actions

to protect Claimants' portfolio from loss during a market correction. Respondent's failure to ensure their employee had a meaningful exit strategy constitutes a breach of such duty.

WHEREFORE Claimants request that an award be entered in their favor against Bad Broker for damages in the approximate amount of $2,102,608.00, plus interest and costs.

COUNT II
MISREPRESENTATION/
OMISSION OF MATERIAL FACTS

16. Claimants reallege the allegations contained in paragraphs 1 through 37.

17. Respondent, through their employee, made untrue statements of material facts and/or omitted or failed to state other material facts. These misrepresentations were at best negligent and at worst either intentional or in reckless disregard for the truth and therefore operated as a fraud upon Claimants in connection with the sale of securities.

18. In particular, Respondent misrepresented and/or failed to advise Claimants of the specific risks that they were subjecting themselves to by investing in the above securities. Respondent's express and/or implied assertions that the investments were suitable for Claimants were false and misleading. Claimants relied on Respondent for professional investment advice which included not merely what investments to purchase, but also to advise against certain strategies.

19. Additionally, Respondent failed to advise Claimants of the risk of continued losses as the market declined; failed to discuss the purchases with Claimants prior to executing the trades; and failed to discuss the impact that the then-current market conditions would have on these investments. Those failures in addition to others referenced above constitute material omissions.

20. Claimants relied upon the misrepresentations and/or omissions of Respondent in deciding the purchase the recommended investments.

21. As a direct and proximate result of the acts and conduct of Respondent's employee, Claimants have been damaged and have suffered losses.

    WHEREFORE Claimants request that an award be entered in their favor against Bad Broker for damages in the approximate amount of $2,102,608.00, plus interest and costs.

COUNT III
VIOLATION OF FLORIDA STATUTE 825.103
EXPLOITATION OF AN ELDERLY PERSON

22. Claimants reallege the allegations contained in paragraphs 1 through 37.

23. Fl. Stat. §825.103(1)(a) states, " 'Exploitation of an elderly person or disabled adult' means: knowingly, by deception … obtaining or using, or endeavoring to obtain or use, an elderly person's … funds, assets, or property with the intent to temporarily or permanently deprive the elderly person … of the use, benefit, or possession of the funds, assets, or property, or to benefit someone other than the elderly person … by a person who: 1. Stands in a position of trust and confidence with the elderly person or disabled adult; or 2. Has a business relationship with the elderly person … ."

24. Respondent's employee obtained Claimants' funds to benefit someone other than the Claimants (to wit: the Respondent brokerage firms). The fees, costs and/or commissions charged to Claimants for the transactions and/or for the maintenance of the account benefited Respondents and permanently deprived Claimants of those funds.

25. Respondent intentionally failed to disclose or explain such fees, charges and/or commissions.

26. Respondent stood in a position of trust and confidence with Claimants and had a business relationship with Claimants.

27. Claimants were over the age of 60 and were therefore classified as "elderly".

28. Respondent, through their employee, knowingly deceived Claimants by making false and misleading statements or by omitting material information necessary to make the statements made not misleading including, but not limited to:

    a. Stating that the investments were safe and the companies were financially sound;

    b. Stating that the investments were suitable for Claimants and complied with their investment objectives and risk tolerance;

c. Failing to advise Claimants of the risk of continued losses as the market declined;

d. Failing to discuss the impact that the then-current market conditions would have on these investments;

e. Failing to explain how these preferred stocks differed from corporate bonds;

f. Failing to inform Claimants that the companies were likely issuing preferred stock instead of bonds because they already had too much debt on their books;

g. Failing to advise Claimants that the call feature of long-maturity preferred stocks negates the benefits of the longer maturity in a falling rate environment, so the holder does not benefit from the price increase that would occur with a non-callable fixed rate security in a falling rate environment;

h. Failing to advise Claimants that, with short maturity preferreds, a company with low-rated credit and a high-yield preferred will likely call in the preferred if its credit status improves, replacing it with a higher-rated bond (that is tax deductible for the issuer) but if the company's credit deteriorates, it will not call in the preferred and the price of the preferred will fall due to the deteriorated credit;

g. Failing to explain that the mutual funds invest primarily in stocks;

h. Failing to inform Claimant that the mutual funds exposed Claimant to the volatility of the stock market;

i. Failing to explain forthrightly the practical impact and potential risks of the course of dealing in which the broker is engaged.

j. Failing to advise Claimants that the specific investments recommended subjected Claimants to more risk than they wanted or that was appropriate for them based on their age, retirement status, income and assets;

k. Failing to advise Claimants that, based on their age, retirement status, income and assets, they were over concentrated in preferred stocks and/or equities;

l. Failing to advise Claimants that, based on their age, retirement status, income and assets, they were over concentrated in financial, real estate and other sectors that had exposure to the subprime mortgage market;

m. Failing to advise Claimants to rebalance the asset allocation of the accounts.

29. Respondent's employee made these, and other, misrepresentations and omissions of material facts with the intent to temporarily or permanently deprive an elderly person of the use, benefit, or possession of the funds. Respondent knew that the value of Claimants' accounts was certain to decline and that Claimants would lose money.

30. Fl. Stat. §772.11(1) (Civil remedy for theft or exploitation) states that, "Any person who proves by clear and convincing evidence that he or she has been injured in any fashion by reason of any violation of … §825.103(1) has a cause of action for threefold the actual damages sustained and, in any such action … and reasonable attorney's fees and court costs in the trial and appellate courts.

31. Respondent's misrepresentations and omissions of material fact constitute a violation of §825.103(1) and Claimants are therefore entitled to recover threefold the actual damages and attorney's fees. Consequently, the Claimants will request that the panel make a specific finding that Respondents violated §825.103so that Claimants may then apply to a court of competent jurisdiction for an award of attorney's fees.

32. Respondent is liable for the actions of its employees on the basis of agency theory or *respondeat superior.*

33. As a direct and proximate result of the acts and conduct of Respondent, Claimants have been damaged and have suffered significant losses. WHEREFORE Claimants request that an award be entered in their favor against Bad Broker for damages in the approximate amount of $2,102,608.00, plus punitive damages equal to three times the actual damages for a total combined damage request of $6,307,824.00 against Bad Broker plus interest, costs and a determination of entitlement to attorneys fees pursuant to Fl. Stat. §772.11.

COUNT IV
FAILURE TO SUPERVISE

34. Claimants reallege the allegations contained in paragraphs 1 through 37.

35. The rules of FINRA require member firms to properly supervise their brokers and their handling of customer accounts and to examine all trading activity taking place therein.

36. FINRA Rule 3010 requires member firms to "establish and maintain a system to supervise the activities of each registered representative and associated persons that is reasonably designed to achieve compliance with applicable securities laws and regulations, and with the [r]ules of [the] Association."

37. Member firms or associated persons can violate the supervisory rules in several circumstances: if the member or individual fails to establish and maintain a supervisory system; fails to describe the operation of that system in written procedures; or, fails to enforce the supervisory system or written supervisory procedures. *Either type of violation can occur in the absence of an underlying rule violation. See* FINRA *Notice to Members* 98-96. Consequently, regardless of whether Respondents had appropriate supervisory procedures in place, if they failed to enforce those procedures, such failure constitutes a violation of the rule.

38. In the case at bar, Respondent's supervisors should have monitored and reviewed all transactions, seeing to it that Claimants were provided with all material information concerning the risks of purchasing these investments and the impact of the then-current market climate and that the trades complied with the stated account objectives for Claimants and were suitable for Claimants and that Respondent's employee was taking appropriate actions to protect his clients from further losses as the market declined.

39. By failing to comply with FINRA and NYSE rules, Respondent breached their contracts and/or breached their fiduciary duties and/or misrepresented themselves to Claimants for which Claimants have suffered damages.

WHEREFORE Claimants request that an award be entered in their favor against Bad Broker for damages in the approximate amount of $2,102,608.00, plus interest and costs.

COUNT V
BREACH OF CONTRACT/UNSUITABILITY

40. Claimants reallege the allegations contained in paragraphs 1 through 37.

41. The contract which Claimants entered into with the Respondent impliedly and/or explicitly stated that Respondent would comply with the state, federal and self regulatory organization laws, rules and regulations.

42. FINRA Rule 2110 states that "A member, in the conduct of his business, shall observe high standards of commercial honor and just and equitable principles of trade."

43. FINRA Rule 2120 states that, "No member shall effect any transaction in, or induce the purchase or sale of, any security by means of any manipulative, deceptive or other fraudulent device or contrivance."

44. FINRA Rule IM-2210-1 states that, "Every member is responsible for determining whether any communication with the public ... complies with all applicable standards, including the requirement that the communication not be misleading. .... These guidelines do not represent an exclusive list of considerations that a member must make in determining whether a communication with the public complies with all applicable standards. (1) Members must ensure that statements are not misleading within the context in which they are made. A statement made in one context may be misleading even though such a statement could be appropriate in another context. An essential test in this regard is the balanced treatment of risks and potential benefits. Member communications should be consistent with the risks of fluctuating prices and the uncertainty of dividends, rates of return and yield inherent to investments." (Emphasis added).

45. FINRA Rule 2310 states that, "In recommending to a customer the purchase, sale or exchange of any security, a member shall have reasonable grounds for believing that the recommendation is suitable for such customer upon the basis of the facts, if any, disclosed by such customer as to his other security holding and as to his financial situation and needs."

46. Furthermore, overconcentration is considered a violation of the

suitability rule (*See, e.g.*, Clinton H. Holland, Jr., 52 S.E.C. 562, 566 (1995) ("The concentration of high risk and speculative securities [in the customer's] account . . . was not suitable."), aff'd 105 F.3d 665 (9th Cir. 1997)). Respondents' recommendations had the effect of over concentrating Claimants in certain types of investments and in certain sectors (i.e., financial and real estate) that were exposed to the subprime mortgage market.

47. Finally, FINRA IM-2310-2(a)(1) states that, "Implicit in all member and registered representative relationships with customers and others is the Fundamental responsibility for fair dealing. Sales efforts must therefore be undertaken only on a basis that can be judged as being within the ethical standards of the Association's Rules, with particular emphasis on the requirement to deal fairly with the public. ... <u>sales efforts must be judged on the basis of whether they can be reasonably said to represent fair treatment for the persons to whom the sales efforts are directed, rather than on the argument that they result in profits to customers.</u>" (Emphasis added).

48. Respondent's recommendations that Claimants purchase the above referenced investments were unsuitable and inappropriate for Claimants.

   a. The specific investments recommended subjected Claimants to more risk than they wanted or that was appropriate for them based on their age, retirement status, income and assets;

   b. The specific investments recommended were not safe and conservative as they should have been for these Claimants' accounts;

   c. The concentration in preferred stocks and equities was an inappropriate strategy for these Claimants based on their age, retirement status, income and assets;

   d. The concentration in financial, real estate and other sectors that had exposure to the subprime mortgage market was an inappropriate strategy for these Claimants based on their age, retirement status, income and assets;

   e. The failure to rebalance the asset allocation was an inappropriate strategy for these Claimants based on their age, retirement status, income and assets.

49. Furthermore, the failure of Respondent to disclose the specific risks associated with these investments as well as the impact that the then-current market conditions would have on these investments constitutes a violation of FINRA Rule 2120 and IM-2210-1. Respondents' sales efforts promoted the yield and potential for higher income without the concomitant balancing of the disclosures of the risks.

50. Respondent's violation of the above referenced rules and laws constitutes a breach of the contract between Claimants and Respondent and Claimants have suffered damages as a result thereof.

WHEREFORE Claimants request that an award be entered in their favor against Bad Broker for damages in the approximate amount of $2,102,608.00, plus interest and costs.

CERTIFICATE OF SERVICE

I HEREBY CERTIFY that a true and correct copy of this Statement of Claim was served by US Mail on the FINRA Dispute Resolution, Inc., One Liberty Plaza, 27th Floor, 165 Broadway, New York, NY 10006 this _____ day of _____, 2009.

Law Firm LLC

By: _____
Lawyer James Doe ESQ.
Florida Bar Number 01234567
2399 NW Blvd.,
Boca Raton, FL 33333
561-241-0000
561-241-0001 Fax
alawyer@mybellsouth.net

Letter for Production list to clients

March 30, 2009

Mark and Theresa Client
5300 Avenue Best Drive
Boca Raton, FL 33484

Subject: CLIENT v Bad Broker; FINRA Case # 09-005xxx

Dear Mr. and Mrs. Client:

Enclosed for your review please find a copy of the Answer to the Statement of Claim filed by the brokerage firm in your case. Your case is now entering the next phase of the arbitration process. About one month from now we will have an arbitration panel appointed and after that we will begin exchanging documents with the brokerage firm.

As with any litigation, both parties to the case ask the other side to produce documents and information. In securities arbitrations such as this, FINRA has compiled a "Discovery Guide". This is a list of documents that are normally produced in most cases. Enclosed for your review is a copy of a list from the Discovery Guide. At this time we are asking you to review this list and begin the process of gathering the documents listed in order to avoid any delay in producing them to the other side.

If you do not have some of the items, do not be alarmed, please simply let us know what you don't have. You are not expected to create documents that don't exist but you will be required to produce documents that are in your "control" (i.e., if your accountant has copies, you would have to get them from him or her even though you may not have them in your own personal possession). We would appreciate if you would send us these documents in the next forty (40) days.

Finally, enclosed please find a draft letter that we would like to have from your doctor. We believe that such a letter will be helpful to your case by demonstrating that you fall within the definition of "elderly" as that term is defined by Florida law. Please provide us with your doctor's name in addition to having him or her prepare the attached letter.

Thank you for your cooperation and if you have any questions, please feel free to contact us.

Very truly yours,
LAW FIRM
Enclosures

DISCOVERY LIST

WHEN a claim is made against a broker or brokerage firm, information is exchanged between the Brokerage firm and the party bringing a claim. Below is a list of items that are often requested by the Broker and Brokerage firm:

DISCOVERY LIST

1) All customer and customer-owned business (including partnership or corporate) federal income tax returns, limited to pages 1 and 2 of Form 1040, Schedules B, D, and E, or the equivalent for any other type of return, for the three years prior to the first transaction at issue in the Statement of Claim through the date the Statement of Claim was filed.

2) Financial statements or similar statements of the customer's assets, liabilities, and/or net worth for the period(s) covering the three years prior to the first transaction at issue in the Statement of Claim through the date the Statement of Claim was filed.

3) Copies of all documents the customer received from the brokerage firm and/or broker and from any entities in which the customer invested through the brokerage firm and/or broker, including monthly statements, opening account forms, confirmations, prospectuses, annual and periodic reports, and correspondence.

4) Account statements and confirmations for accounts maintained at securities firms other than the respondent brokerage firm for the three years prior to the first transaction at issue in the Statement of Claim through the date the Statement of Claim was filed.

5) All agreements, forms, information, or documents relating to the account(s) at issue signed by or provided by the customer to the brokerage firm and/or broker.

6) All account analyses and reconciliations prepared by or for the customer relating to the account(s) at issue.

7) All notes, including entries in diaries or calendars, relating to the account(s) at issue.

8) All recordings and notes of telephone calls or conversations about the customer's account(s) at issue that occurred between the broker and the customer (and any person acting on behalf of the customer).

9) All correspondence between the customer (and any person acting on behalf of the customer) and the brokerage firm and/or broker relating to the account(s) at issue.

10) Previously prepared written statements by persons with knowledge of the facts and circumstances related to the account(s) at issue, including those by accountants, tax advisors, financial planners, other Associated Person(s), and any other third party.

11) All prior complaints by or on behalf of the customer involving securities matters and the brokerage firm's and/or broker's response(s).

12) Complaints/Statements of Claim and Answers filed in all civil actions involving securities matters and securities arbitration proceedings in which the customer has been a party, and all final decisions and awards entered in these matters.

13) All documents showing action taken by the customer to limit losses in the transaction(s) at issue.

14) Documents sufficient to show the customer's ownership in or control over any business entity, including general and limited partnerships and closely held corporations.

15) Copy of the customer's resume or, if you do not have a resume, a description of your complete educational and employment background.

17) Written documents relied upon by the customer in making the investment decision(s) at issue.

(For Unauthorized Trading Claims, Also produce:)

18) Copies of all telephone records, including telephone logs, evidencing telephone contact between the customer and the brokerage firm/broker.

19) All documents relied upon by the customer to show that the transaction(s) at issue was made without his/her knowledge or consent.

Doctor's Letter

(This example is to be typed on the doctor's Letter Head)

To Whom it May Concern:

Please accept this letter as an opinion as a result of my examination and on-going care of _____.
It is my opinion within a reasonable degree of medical probability that _____ is suffering from the infirmities of aging as manifested by advanced age or other physical, mental or emotional dysfunctioning to the extent that the ability of this patient is impaired to some extent.

Very truly yours,

Dr._____

Request for Production
Cover Letter to Attorney

July 9, 2009
Clark H. Lawyer, Esq.,
2800 SW Avenue
Miami, FL 33333

Subject: Client v. Bad Broker.
FINRA Case #09-00011

Dear Ms. Lawyer:
Please find the enclosed Claimant's Request for Production of Documents
and Information. Thank you for your cooperation with this matter.
Please feel to contact me should you have any questions or concerns.
Sincerely,
Attorney at Law

Request for Production

BEFORE THE ARBITRATION TRIBUNAL OF
FINRA DISPUTE RESOLUTION, INC

MAY CLIENT,   )
   Claimant,   ) FINRA Case #11-0001
)
vs.   )
)
Bad Broker,   )
   Respondent.   )
_____   )

CLAIMANT'S REQUEST FOR PRODUCTION OF DOCUMENTS AND INFORMATION

COMES NOW, MARY CLIENT (hereinafter referred to as "Mrs. C" or "Claimant") by and through her undersigned counsel and files this Request for Production of Documents and Information from Respondent, BAD BROKER INC., (hereinafter referred to as "BAD BROKER" or "Respondent") and states as follows:

DEFINITIONS

The following definitions apply to this request:

1. When used in this Request the plural form shall be substituted for the singular where appropriate and shall have the same meaning as defined below. Similarly, the masculine pronouns shall be substituted for the feminine, and the singular for the plural, and shall apply equally and have the same meaning.

2. The term "Document" refers to any printed, written, taped, recorded, graphic, computerized printout, electronic or optical storage media, or other tangible matter, from whatever source, however produced or reproduced, whether in draft form or otherwise, whether sent or received, or neither, including, but not limited to, the original, a copy (if the original is not available), and all non-identical copies (whether different from the original because of notes made on or attached to such copy or otherwise) of any and all writings, correspondence, letters, telegrams, cables, telexes, facsimiles (fax), contracts, proposals, agreements, minutes, acknowledgements, notes, memoranda, evaluations, critiques, assessments, studies, analyses, projections, work papers, books, forecasts, appraisals, papers, records, reports, diaries, statements, questionnaires, schedules, computer programs or data, books of account, calendars, graphs, charts, transcripts, tapes or recordings, photographs, pictures or film, ledgers, registers, work sheets, summaries, digests, financial statements, and all other information where data, records, or compilations, including underlying, supporting or preparatory material now in your possession, custody or control, or available to you, your counsel, accountants, programmers, contractors, agents,

representatives, or associates. "Document" specifically includes documents kept by individuals in their desks, at home or elsewhere.

3. "Corporate Records" refers to articles of incorporation, bylaws, corporation minutes, and related documents.

4. "Copy" when used in reference to a document, means any color, or black and white, reproduction of a document, regardless of whether the reproduction is made by means of facsimile, carbon paper, pressure sensitive paper, xerography, electronic files including ".pdf" files, word processing documents (i.e., Word, Wordperfect, and the like), electronic spreadsheets (i.e., "Excel" files), or other means or process.

5. The term "Communication" or "Communicate" means any writing, or oral conversation, including, but not limited to, telephone conversations and meetings, letters, telegraphic and telex communications, electronic mail (e-mail), and includes all information relating to all oral communications and documents (as previously defined) whether or not any such document, or the information contained therein, was transmitted by its author to any other person.

6. "Person" shall mean all natural persons ("individual") and entities, (including subsidiaries, departments, divisions, and committees thereof) and including without limitation: corporations, companies, partnerships, limited partnerships, joint ventures, proprietorships, trusts, estates, associations, any government or political subdivision thereof, or government body, commission board, public agencies, departments, bureaus and boards.

7. "You", "Your" or "Respondent" shall refer to BAD BROKER its assignors; merged, consolidated or acquired predecessors or successors; divisions, affiliates, units, and subsidiaries, whether or not wholly owned; including all other persons acting or purporting to act on its behalf; experts, persons consulted concerning any factual matter or matters of opinion relating to any of the facts or issues involved in this action, and, unless privileged, any attorneys representing Respondent.

8. "Relating to", "relate to", regarding" and "concerning" shall be construed in their broader sense and shall mean directly or indirectly describing, setting forth, discussing, mentioning, commenting upon, supporting, contradicting, or referring to the subject or topic in question, either in full or in part.

9. "Identify" when used in reference to:

   a. an individual, shall mean to state his full name and present or last known address (including zip code), phone number, and present or last known position or business affiliation (designating which), and the job description.

   b. a corporation, company, partnership, limited partnership, joint venture, proprietorship, trust, estate, and association, shall mean to state its full name and present or last known address (designating which) and to state the name and address of each person within the entity likely to have knowledge of the relationship between that entity and Respondent as well as all officers, directors, partners, general partners, trustees, administrators or executors, or owners of a controlling interest in such entity.

10. "Data" shall mean to state: in the case of a document, the date, author, sender, recipient, type of document or some other means of identifying it and its present location and custodian; in the case of oral communication, the date, the parties to the communication, and the nature of the communication.

10. "BAD BROKER" shall mean "BAD BROKER INC." including any subsidiaries, affiliates, segments or divisions, and any present or former officers, directors, employees, agents, representatives, independent contractors, or other persons acting on its behalf.

11. "The broker" shall mean BAD BROKER.

12. "Sales Literature" shall mean any document or electronic communication drafted, designed, printed, or otherwise made available to BAD brokers or used by brokers or any personnel, regardless of whether it was approved, formally or informally or in any other manner by BAD BROKER, for the purpose or intent of soliciting interest in, describing or actually selling any BAD BROKER product or service.

13. "Sales Practices" shall mean any practice, policy, tactic, procedure, strategy, plan or approach taught to, advocated by or used by any BAD BROKER personnel, regardless of whether it was approved, formally, informally or in any other manner by BAD BROKER, for the purpose

or intent of soliciting interest in or actually selling any BAD BROKER product or service.

14. "Regulatory Agency" shall mean any federal, state and/or local governmental agency, and/or Self Regulatory Organization, including any division, employee or agent thereof, responsible for monitoring, supervising, regulating and/or reviewing the advertising, policies, procedures, conduct, management, and operations of brokerage firms including BAD BROKER.

15. The relevant time period for the following requests, unless otherwise indicated, shall mean from October 2007 to the date of full compliance with the request to produce.

INSTRUCTIONS

1. Each request herein for a document contemplates production thereof in full, without abbreviation or expurgation, and calls for production of all copies that have notes or other written material or markings not appearing on other copies.

2. **Claimant will execute any confidentiality agreement for documents for which a claim of privilege is asserted and will affirm that such documents will only be used within the confines of this arbitration proceeding and will return any copies or originals of such documents to Respondent.**

3. If a claim of privilege is asserted to any document requested to be produced herein (privilege as used herein shall include attorneys' work product), such document shall be sufficiently described so that Claimant can bring the question of privilege before the Chairman of the arbitration panel. Documents shall be deemed to be adequately described for this purpose if the following data are provided: (1) the type of document, e.g., letter or memorandum; (2) the general subject matter of the document including a brief description or summary of the contents of the document sufficient to explain the privilege invoked; (3) the date of the document; (4) the author, addressee, and any other recipient of the document, and, where not apparent, the relationship of the author, addressee, and any other recipient to each other; (5) the name and position of each person, other than attorneys representing any of the Respondents in connection with this claim, to

whom the contents of the document have been communicated by copy, exhibition, reading or substantial summarization; and (6) the identity of each person who has custody of a copy of the document.

4. In producing documents responsive to this Request, organize and label the documents so as to correspond to the individual document requests set forth below.

5. This Request is considered to be continuing in character and nature. Therefore, you are required promptly to produce additional documents if you obtain further, additional, or different information or documents prior to the trial or hearing in this matter.

PLACE OF PRODUCTION

You are requested to produce the documents designated herein at the offices of LAWYER LLC, 200 NW Blvd., Boca Raton, FL 33333, within sixty (60) days of this request or such other time period as may be ordered by the arbitrator(s) assigned to this matter.

REQUEST FOR DOCUMENTS

1. To the extent Respondent has not already done so, produce all documents specified in the FINRA Discovery Guide, List Numbers 1, 5, 7, 9, 11, and 13 as required by FINRA Arbitration Rule 12506.

2. Any and all financial profiles or questionnaires completed by or on behalf of Claimant for Respondent or by the broker, or on behalf of the broker, Respondent (or any employee of Respondent), for Claimant, including any preliminary drafts and final versions.

3. All portions of the branch correspondence file referencing Claimant, Claimant's account(s) or any of the securities recommended to and/or purchased by or for Claimant by the broker.

4. All margin and/or maintenance calls, front and back, that were created and generated in connection with any and all transactions made in Claimant's account(s).

5. All confirmations for the Claimant's transactions.

6. All order tickets, front and back, that were created in connection with all purchase and sales orders in Claimant's account(s). This request

includes all cancellation and "as of" tickets, and any documents or memoranda that address the order's cancellation, withdrawal or error.

7. Any profit and loss statements prepared in connection with Claimant's account(s).

8. All request forms submitted by the broker or any other employee of Respondent that were used to generate correspondence to Claimant.

9. All research and/or due diligence files relating to the investments recommended to the Claimant by Respondent's employees. More particularly, regarding each specific investment identified in the Statement of Claim, this request seeks production of any and all documents (including, but not limited to, memos, summaries, reports) evidencing "due diligence" conducted by:

   a. BAD BROKER (or any employee thereof);
   b. Any manager, supervisor or compliance personnel with supervisory authority over the broker; and/or
   c. The broker,

   In connection with this paragraph, the term "due diligence" refers to a review and analysis of an investment with respect to its past and anticipated performance taking into consideration all factors that a reasonable person would consider material including, but not necessarily limited to: underlying financial condition; stability; earnings; debt; management; SEC filings; and market conditions likely to affect such investment's performance.

10. Any and all recommendations, notes, memoranda or other written documents produced by BAD BROKER that provided research or recommendations on the securities bought and sold in the Claimant's account(s). Such material would include but not be limited to suggested buy and sell recommendations of BAD BROKER and its agents or subsidiaries.

11. Any daily calendars, day-timers, diaries, telephone call logbooks and/or their functional equivalent, containing entries describing or noting the activities or telephone calls of the broker, and/or any other employee in the branch office, since inception of Claimant's account(s) to date that relate in any way to the Claimant's account(s).

12. Any and all documents relating to conversations (regardless of whether such conversations were in-person, telephonically, or via written correspondence) with Claimant that specifically evidence discussions of:

   a. The risks of the particular investment(s) being recommended (regardless of whether or not Claimant actually purchased the investment);
   b. The risks of the particular investment(s) that Claimant actually purchased;
   c. Diversification;
   d. How the particular investment(s) being recommended met Claimant's investment objectives;
   e. Income;
   f. Preferred stocks as compared with corporate or municipal bonds;
   g. Alternative investments to those being recommended.

13. Copies of all telephone records (local and long distance) from the branch office as well as the broker's cellular (or mobile) telephones and the broker's home telephones, including, but not limited to, telephone logs and telephone bills that evidence telephone contact between the Claimant and the broker, or any other employee of Respondent from the date specified in paragraph 16 of the Definitions section above to the present (inclusive).

14. The telephone numbers and long distance carriers for the Respondent branch office where Claimant maintained their account(s).

15. The telephone numbers and long distance carriers (both work, home and cellular) for the broker and/or any other employee in the branch office where Claimant maintained their account(s) who had any telephone contact with the Claimant.

16. All tape recordings or documents relating to any conversations between or among Respondent's employees, excluding counsel, about or with Claimant.

17. The full and complete personnel files of the broker.

18. All Forms RE-3, U-4, and U-5, for all employees in the Respondent's branch office where Claimant maintained their account(s) including all

amendments, all customer complaints identified in such forms, and all customer complaints of a similar nature to those raised in the Claim.

19. All supervisory logs, reviews and/or reports from or pertaining to the branch office where Claimant maintained their account(s) during the period from the date of the broker's employment to the present.

20. Records of disciplinary action taken against the broker by any regulator or employer.

21. All sales literature, prospectuses, risk disclosure statements, brochures, pamphlets, literature, wires, handwritten notes, audiotapes, video-tapes or other information or documents given, mailed or shown to Claimant that recommend, explained, discussed or related in any way to any of the services or products offered by or recommended by Respondents including, but not limited to: due diligence; on-going portfolio monitoring; portfolio analyses; auditing of performance, transactions, and positions.

22. All internal sales literature, memoranda, prospectus, risk disclosure statements, correspondence, brochures, pamphlets, literature, audio-tapes, videotapes or information distributed to BAD brokers or made available to BAD BROKER customers or the general public, whether or not shown to Claimant, which recommended, explained, discussed or related to any of the services or products offered by or recommended by Respondents.

23. Any and all documents that evidence BAD BROKER policies, rules, guidelines, or suggestions concerning appropriate allocations for retirees in specific types of investments (i.e., common stock, preferred stock, bonds, mutual funds, closed-end funds, etc..).

24. Any and all documents that evidence BAD BROKER policies, rules, guidelines, or suggestions concerning appropriate allocations for retirees in specific market sectors (i.e., consumer cyclical; technology; financial; transportation; etc…).

25. Any and all documents that evidence BAD BROKER policies, rules, guidelines, or suggestions concerning appropriate specific investments for retirees.

26. All documents reflecting compensation of any kind, including commis-sions, from all sources generated by the broker for the period specified in paragraph 16 in the Definitions section above to the present.

Respondents may redact all information identifying customers who are not parties to the action, except that BROKER shall provide at least the last four digits of the non-party customer account numbers for each transaction.

27. Documents sufficient to describe or set forth the basis upon which the broker was compensated during the period specified in paragraph 16 in the Definitions section above to the present, including:

   a. any bonus or incentive program; and
   b. all compensation and commission schedules showing compensation received or to be received based upon volume, type of product sold, nature of trade (e.g., agency v. principal), etc.

28. A description of any and all fees paid to BROKER by other individuals or entities in connection with the purchases made by Claimant. This request includes, but is not limited to: commissions; rebates; or other "soft dollar" forms of compensation.

29. Any and all documents detailing the fees paid by the Claimant to BROKER on each specific investment purchased and the total amount of such fees paid by Claimant.

30. All documents relating to the Sales Literature or Sales Practices taught to, or used by, or made available to, the broker and any other employees, including, but not limited to, any sales agent, registered representative, supervisor or manager in the office of BROKER in which the broker was employed.

31. A full and complete list of each employee of the office, including the name, address, and telephone number and employment position.

32. All documents that evidence, indicate, or refer to any lawsuit or claim against BROKER and/or the broker by any customer during the past five (5) years.

33. All documents that evidence, indicate, or refer to any lawsuit or claim against BROKER relating to alleged acts or omissions of a BROKER employee during the past five (5) years.

34. All periodic and annual records of ranking the commission/sales performance of all employees in the office during the period of the broker's employment through the present date.

35. Any and all statement(s) of personal account(s) of the broker from the date of his employment to present, including personal, joint or trust account(s).

36. A list of all other clients of the branch office where Claimant maintained their account(s) who purchased the same investments that are the subject of the Statement of Claim.

37. A list of all other clients of the broker who purchased the same investments that are the subject of the Statement of Claim.

38. A list of all transactions executed in the branch office in the securities bought and sold in the Claimant's account(s) during the same period that these securities were being bought, sold or held in the account(s) of the Claimant.

39. A list of all securities that were bought and sold in the account(s) of the Claimant and in which BROKER either acted as a market maker or held the security in its corporate account(s).

40. Copies of all transactions in BROKER's corporate account(s) in securities held in the account(s) of the Claimant during the same period those securities were held by Claimant.

41. All of BROKER complaint files referencing the broker, or any employees in the branch office including, but not limited to, all correspondence, notes, memoranda, drafts, records or other documents.

42. Any and all documents Respondents have received or will receive during the course of this proceeding in response to a subpoena issued in this proceeding.

43. All non-attorney/client privileged materials maintained in the Compliance Department or in the branch office or any other office of BROKER on the review of the Claimant's account(s).

44. All documents that you intend to introduce as exhibits at the arbitration hearing on this matter.

45. All documents that support or relate to your defenses and/or your Answer to the Claim.

46. Any report or other written documents prepared by any expert retained by or on behalf of BROKER in connection with this dispute.

47. The most current annual report of BROKER.

REQUEST FOR INFORMATION

48. State the name, current business address, or last known address of employment for the Operations Manager and Branch Manager for BROKER's branch office during the time period Claimant maintained account(s) at said office.

49. State the name, current business address, or last known address for the BROKER employee who had immediate supervisory responsibilities for the broker.

50. State name of the BROKER compliance department individual with responsibility over the broker and/or the branch office where Claimant maintained their account(s).

51. Identify the name, title, and current address of any and all individuals whose job responsibilities include or included receiving and/or responding to customer complaints regarding BROKER or any of its employees.

52. All documents relating to the duties and/or responsibilities of all individuals identified in paragraph numbers 48 through 51.

53. Identify all persons with any knowledge of the facts supporting Respondents' claims, as alleged in the Answers.

54. Identify all sources of information that BROKER provided, or made available to, the broker concerning:

    a. Prior market "crashes" (for example, 1989 and 2001 market "corrections");
    b. Market volatility;
    c. Sub-prime mortgages and their impact on financial institutions;
    d. Lehman Brother's financial troubles in 2007 and 2008;
    e. Each of the investments identified in the Statement of Claim;

55. All non-attorney/client privileged documents, including minutes of any meetings, concerning any complaints from customers regarding BROKER and/or the broker and what actions BROKER took to address such complaints including agendas, minutes, scripts, attendance records or recordings.

56. All documents relating to the review and/or approval by BROKER

legal department, compliance department, regulatory agency or any other person or department of all sales literature or advertisements concerning BROKER.

CERTIFICATE OF SERVICE

I HEREBY CERTIFY that a true and correct copy of this Request for Production was served by U.S. Mail on counsel for Respondent Clark Lawyer, Esq., , this _____ day of _____, 2011.

LawFirm LLC

By: _____
Law Firm
Florida Bar Number 000333
12300 NW Blvd., Suite 777
Boca Raton, FL 33333
561-200-0000
561-200-0001 Fax
Lawyer@mybellsouth.net

Submission Agreement

FINRA ARBITRATION Submission Agreement
Claimant(s)
In the Matter of the Arbitration Between

Name(s) of Claimant(s)
and
Name(s) of Respondent(s)

1. The undersigned parties ("parties") hereby submit the present matter in controversy, as set forth in the attached statement of claim, answers, and all related cross claims, counterclaims and/or third-party claims which may be asserted, to arbitration in accordance with the FINRA By-Laws, Rules, and Code of Arbitration Procedure.
2. The parties hereby state that they or their representative(s) have read the procedures and rules of FINRA relating to arbitration, and the parties agree to be bound by these procedures and rules.
3. The parties agree that in the event a hearing is necessary, such hearing shall be held at a time and place as may be designated by the Director of Arbitration or the arbitrator(s). The parties further agree and understand that the arbitration will be conducted in accordance with the FINRA Code of Arbitration Procedure.
4. The parties agree to abide by and perform any award(s) rendered pursuant to this Submission Agreement. The parties further agree that a judgment and any interest due thereon, may be entered upon such award(s) and, for these purposes, the parties hereby voluntarily consent to submit to the jurisdiction of any court of competent jurisdiction which may properly enter such judgment.

The parties hereto have signed and acknowledged the foregoing Submission Agreement.

Claimant Name (please print)

_____

Claimant's Signature Date _____

State capacity if other than individual (e.g., executor, trustee or corporate officer)
Claimant Name (please print)

Claimant's Signature Date
State capacity if other than individual (e.g., executor, trustee or corporate officer)

WHO IS "FINRA"

In the United States FINRA is the largest independent regulator of securities firms and Brokers. FINRA is also known as The Financial Industry Regulatory Authority.

FINRA website states that FINRA "oversees nearly 4,850 brokerage firms, about 173,000 branch offices and approximately 647,000 registered securities representatives." **FINRA uses the term** "registered securities representatives" to describe brokers and other registered investment advisors.

In the first edition of this book the NASD rules were discussed . Prior to 2007 most disputes between a Broker and the investor were resolved in binding arbitration using the NASD rules. In July of 2007 the consolidation of NASD and the member regulation, enforcement and arbitration functions of the New York Stock Exchange resulted in FINRA.

If you go to the FINRA website at http://www.finra.org you will learn that FINRA is involved with many aspects of the securities business including:

Registering Brokers and brokerage firms
Educating investors, Brokers and brokerage firms
Writing rules
Enforcing FINRA rules and the federal securities laws.

FINRA has more than two thousand employees and operates from Washington, DC, New York, NY, and 15 District Offices around the country.

YOUR BROKER'S REPUTATION WITH FINRA

You can look up for free the background and reputation of your broker or brokerage firm using "FINRA BrokerCheck®"

http://www.finra.org/Investors/ToolsCalculators/BrokerCheck/index.htm

THIS online service is at the most requested page on the FINRA website. The information includes the securities industry online registration and licensing database on more than six hundred thousand brokers and more than five thousand brokerage firms/securities dealers. The Information online has information on thousands of formerly registered firms and brokers.

CODE OF ARBITRATION PROCEDURE OF THE FINANCIAL INDUSTRY REGULATORY AUTHORITY (FINRA)

© 2009 FINRA. All rights reserved. FINRA is a registered trademark of the Financial Industry Regulatory Authority, Inc.
Reprinted with permission from FINRA.

12000. CODE OF ARBITRATION PROCEDURE FOR CUSTOMER DISPUTES

PART I INTERPRETIVE MATERIAL, DEFINITIONS, ORGANIZATION AND AUTHORITY

IM-12000. Failure to Act Under Provisions of Code of Arbitration Procedure for Customer Disputes

The Customer Code applies to claims filed on or after April 16, 2007. In addition, the list selection provisions of the Customer Code apply to previously filed claims in which a list of arbitrators must be generated after April 16, 2007; in these cases, however, the claim will continue to be governed by the remaining provisions of the old Code unless all parties agree to proceed under the new Code.

It may be deemed conduct inconsistent with just and equitable principles of trade and a violation of Rule 2010 for a member or a person associated with a member to:

a. fail to submit a dispute for arbitration under the Code as required by the Code;

b. fail to comply with any injunctive order issued pursuant to the Code;

c. fail to appear or to produce any document in his possession or control as directed pursuant to provisions of the Code;

d. fail to honor an award, or comply with a written and executed settlement agreement, obtained in connection with an arbitration submitted for disposition pursuant to the rules applicable to the arbitration of disputes before FINRA or other dispute resolution forum selected by the parties where timely motion has not been made to vacate or modify such award pursuant to applicable law; or

e. fail to comply with a written and executed settlement agreement, obtained in connection with a mediation submitted for disposition pursuant to the procedures specified by FINRA.

All awards shall be honored by a cash payment to the prevailing party of the exact dollar amount stated in the award. Awards may not be honored by crediting the prevailing party's account with the dollar amount of the award, unless authorized by the express terms of the award or consented to in writing by the parties. Awards shall be honored upon receipt thereof, or within such other time period as may be prescribed by the award.

It may be deemed conduct inconsistent with just and equitable principles of trade and a violation of Rule 2010 for a member to require associated persons to waive the arbitration of disputes contrary to the provisions of the Code of Arbitration Procedure.

Amended by SR-FINRA-2008-057 eff. Dec. 15, 2008.
Amended by SR-FINRA-2008-021 eff. Dec. 15, 2008.
Amended by SR-NASD-2007-026 eff. April 16, 2007
Adopted by SR-NASD-2003-158 eff. April 16 2007

12100. Definitions

The Customer Code applies to claims filed on or after April 16, 2007. In addition, the list selection provisions of the Customer Code apply to previously filed claims in which a list of arbitrators must be generated after April 16, 2007; in these cases, however, the

claim will continue to be governed by the remaining provisions of the old Code unless all parties agree to proceed under the new Code.

Unless otherwise defined in the Code, terms used in the Rules and interpretive material, if defined in the FINRA By-Laws, shall have the meaning as defined in the FINRA By-Laws.

(a) Associated Person

The term "associated person" or "associated person of a member" means a person associated with a member, as that term is defined in paragraph (r).

(b) Award

An award is a document stating the disposition of a case.

(c) Board

The term "Board" means the Board of Directors of FINRA Dispute Resolution, Inc.

(d) Claim

The term "claim" means an allegation or request for relief.

(e) Claimant

The term "claimant" means a party that files the statement of claim that initiates an arbitration under Rule 12302.

(f) Code

The term "Code" means the Code of Arbitration Procedure for Customer Disputes. For disputes involving only industry parties, see the Code of Arbitration Procedure for Industry Disputes.

(g) Counterclaim

The term "counterclaim" means a claim asserted against a claimant by a respondent.

(h) Cross Claim

The term "cross claim" means a claim asserted by a respondent against another alreadynamed respondent.

(i) Customer

A customer shall not include a broker or dealer.

(j) Day

Except as otherwise provided, the term "day" means calendar day. If a deadline specified in the Code falls on a Saturday, Sunday or any FINRA holiday, the deadline is extended until the next business day.

(k) Director

The term "Director" means the Director of FINRA Dispute Resolution. Unless the Code provides that the Director may not delegate a specific function, the term includes FINRA staff to whom the Director has delegated authority.

(l) Dispute

(m) Hearing

(n) Hearing Session

The term "dispute" means a dispute, claim or controversy. A dispute may consist of one or more claims.

The term "hearing" means the hearing on the merits of an arbitration under Rule 12600. The term "hearing session" means any meeting between the parties and arbitrator(s) of four hours or less, including a hearing or a prehearing conference.

(o) Member

For purposes of the Code, the term "member" means any broker or dealer admitted to membership in FINRA, whether or not the membership has been terminated or cancelled; and any broker or dealer admitted to membership in a self-regulatory organization that, with FINRA consent, has required its members to arbitrate pursuant to the Code and/or to be treated as members of FINRA for purposes of the Code, whether or not the membership has been terminated or cancelled.

(p) Non-Public Arbitrator

The term "non-public arbitrator" means a person who is otherwise qualified to serve as an arbitrator and:

(1) is, or within the past five years, was:

    (a) associated with, including registered through, a broker or a dealer
(including a government securities broker or dealer or a municipal securities dealer) ;

    (b) registered under the Commodity Exchange Act;

(c) a member of a commodities exchange or a registered futures association; or

(d) associated with a person or firm registered under the Commodity Exchange Act;

(2) is retired from, or spent a substantial part of a career engaging in, any of the business activities listed in paragraph (p) (1);

(3) is an attorney, accountant, or other professional who has devoted 20 percent or more of his or her professional work, in the last two years, to clients who are engaged in any of the business activities listed in paragraph (p) (1); or

(4) is an employee of a bank or other financial institution and effects transactions in securities, including government or municipal securities, and commodities futures or options or supervises or monitors the compliance with the securities and commodities laws of employees who engage in such activities.

For purposes of this rule, the term "professional work" shall not include mediation services performed by mediators who are also arbitrators, provided that the mediator acts in the capacity of a mediator and does not represent a party in the mediation.

(q) Panel

The term "panel" means the arbitration panel, whether it consists of one or more arbitrators.

(r) Person Associated with a Member

The term "person associated with a member" means:

1. A natural person registered under the Rules of FINRA; or

2. A sole proprietor, partner, officer, director, or branch manager of a member, or a natural person occupying a similar status or performing similar functions, or a natural person engaged in the investment banking or securities business who is directly or indirectly controlling or controlled by a member, whether or not any such person is registered or exempt from registration with FINRA under the By-Laws or the Rules of FINRA.

For purposes of the Code, a person formerly associated with a member is a person associated with a member.

(s) Pleadings

A pleading is a statement describing a party's causes of action or defenses. Documents that are considered pleadings are: a statement of claim, an answer, a counterclaim, a cross claim, a third party claim, and any replies.

(t) Prehearing Conference

The term "prehearing conference" means any hearing session, including an Initial Prehearing Conference, that takes place before the hearing on the merits begins.

(u) Public Arbitrator

The term "public arbitrator" means a person who is otherwise qualified to serve as an arbitrator and:

1. is not engaged in the conduct or activities described in paragraphs (p) (1) (4) ;
2. was not engaged in the conduct or activities described in paragraphs (p) (1) (4) for a total of 20 years or more;
3. is not an investment adviser;
4. is not an attorney, accountant, or other professional whose firm derived 10 percent or more of its annual revenue in the past two years from any persons or entities listed in paragraphs (p) (1) -(4) ;
5. is not an attorney, accountant, or other professional whose firm derived $50,000 or more in annual revenue in the past two years from professional services rendered to any persons or entities listed inparagraph (p) (1) relating to any customer disputes concerning an investment account or transaction, including but not limited to, law firm fees, accounting firm fees, and consulting fees;
6. is not employed by, and is not the spouse or an immediate fami-lymember of a person who is employed by, an entity that directly orindirectly controls, is controlled by, or is under common control with, any partnership, corporation, or other organization that is engaged in the securities business;
7. is not a director or officer of, and is not the spouse or an immediate

family member of a person who is a director or officer of, an entity that directly or indirectly controls, is controlled by, or is under common control with, any partnership, corporation, or other organization that is engaged in the securities business; and

8. is not the spouse or an immediate family member of a person who is engaged in the conduct or activities described in paragraphs (p) (1)-(4). For purposes of this rule, the term immediate family member means:

(A) a person's parent, stepparent, child, or stepchild;
(B) a member of a person's household;
(C) an individual to whom a person provides financial support of more than 50 percent of his or her annual income; or
(D) a person who is claimed as a dependent for federal income tax purposes.

For purposes of this rule, the term "revenue" shall not include mediation fees received by mediators who are also arbitrators, provided that the mediator acts in the capacity of a mediator and does not represent a party in the mediation.

v. Respondent
The term "respondent" means a party against whom a statement of claim or third party claim has been filed. A claimant against whom a counterclaim has been filed is not a respondent for purposes of the Code.

w. Statement of Claim
The term "statement of claim" means the initial or amended claim filed by the party or parties initiating the arbitration.

x. Submission Agreement
The term "Submission Agreement" means the FINRA Submission Agreement. The FINRA Submission Agreement is a document that parties must sign at the outset of an arbitration in which they agree to submit to arbitration under the Code.

y. Third Party Claim
The term "third party claim" means a claim asserted against a party

not already named in the statement of claim or any other previous pleading.

Amended by SR-FINRA-2008-031. eff. Feb. 9, 2009.
Amended by SR-FINRA-2008-021 eff. Dec. 15, 2008.
Amended by SR-NASD-2007-021 eff. June 9, 2008.
Amended by SR-NASD-2007-038 eff. June 14, 2007.
Adopted by SR-NASD-2003-158 eff. April 16, 2007.

Selected Notices to Members: 07-07, 08-22, 08-57, 09-04.

12101. Applicability of Code and Incorporation by Reference

The Customer Code applies to claims filed on or after April 16, 2007. In addition, the list selection provisions of the Customer Code apply to previously filed claims in which a list of arbitrators must be generated after April 16, 2007; in these cases, however, the claim will continue to be governed by the remaining provisions of the old Code unless all parties agree to proceed under the new Code.

a. Applicability of Code
The Code applies to any dispute between a customer and a member or associated person of a member that is submitted to arbitration under Rule 12200 or 12201.
b. Incorporation by Reference
When a dispute is submitted to arbitration under the Code pursuant to an arbitration agreement, the Code is incorporated by reference into the agreement.

Amended by SR-FINRA-2008-021 eff. Dec. 15, 2008.
Adopted by SR-NASD-2003-158 eff. April 16, 2007.

Selected Notices: 07-07, 08-57.

12102. National Arbitration and Mediation Committee

The Customer Code applies to claims filed on or after April 16,

2007. In addition, the list selection provisions of the Customer Code apply to previously filed claims in which a list of arbitrators must be generated after April 16, 2007; in these cases, however, the claim will continue to be governed by the remaining provisions of the old Code unless all parties agree to proceed under the new Code.

a. Pursuant to Section III of the Plan of Allocation and Delegation of Functions by FINRA to Subsidiaries ("Delegation Plan"), the Board shall appoint a National Arbitration and Mediation Committee ("NAMC").

    1. The NAMC shall consist of no fewer than 10 and no more than 25 members. At least 50 percent of the NAMC shall be Non-Industry members.
    2. The Chairperson of the Board shall name the chairperson of the NAMC.

b. Pursuant to the Delegation Plan, the NAMC shall have the authority to recommend rules, regulations, procedures and amendments relating to arbitration, mediation, and other dispute resolution matters to the Board. The NAMC shall also establish and maintain rosters of neutrals composed of persons from within and outside of the securities industry. All matters recommended by the NAMC to the Board must have been approved by a quorum, which shall consist of a majority of the NAMC, including at least 50 percent of the Non-Industry committee members. If at least 50 percent of the Non-Industry committee members are either (I) present at or (II) have filed a waiver of attendance for a meeting after receiving an agenda prior to such meeting, the requirement that at least 50 percent of the Non-Industry committee members be present to constitute the quorum shall be waived. The NAMC has such other power and authority as is necessary to carry out the purposes of the Code.

c. The NAMC may meet as frequently as necessary, but must meet at least once a year.

Amended by SR-FINRA-2009-003 eff. Jan. 8, 2009.

Amended by SR-FINRA-2008-021 eff. Dec. 15, 2008.
Amended by SR-NASD-2007-026 eff. April 16, 2007.
Adopted by SR-NASD-2003-158 eff. April 16, 2007.

Selected Notices: 07-07, 08-57.

12103. *Director of Dispute Resolution*

The Customer Code applies to claims filed on or after April 16, 2007. In addition, the list selection provisions of the Customer Code apply to previously filed claims in which a list of arbitrators must be generated after April 16, 2007; in these cases, however, the claim will continue to be governed by the remaining provisions of the old Code unless all parties agree to proceed under the new Code.

a. The Board shall appoint a Director of Dispute Resolution. The Director shall perform all the administrative duties relating to arbitrations submitted under the Code. The Director may delegate his or her duties when it is appropriate, unless the Code provides otherwise.
b. The Director shall consult with the NAMC at the NAMC's request.
c. The President of FINRA Dispute Resolution may perform the Director's duties. If the Director is unable to perform his or her duties, the President of FINRA Dispute Resolution may appoint an interim Director.

Amended by SR-FINRA-2008-021 eff. Dec. 15, 2008.
Adopted by SR-NASD-2003-158 eff. April 16, 2007.

Selected Notices: 07-07, 08-57.

12104. *Effect of Arbitration on FINRA Regulatory Activities*

The Customer Code applies to claims filed on or after April 16, 2007. In addition, the list selection provisions of the Customer Code apply to previously filed claims in which a list of arbitrators must be generated after April 16, 2007; in these cases, however, the

claim will continue to be governed by the remaining provisions of the old Code unless all parties agree to proceed under the new Code.

a. Submitting a dispute to arbitration under the Code does not limit or preclude any right, action or determination by FINRA that it would otherwise be authorized to adopt, administer or enforce.

b. Only at the conclusion of an arbitration, any arbitrator may refer to FINRA for disciplinary investigation any matter that has come to the arbitrator's attention during and in connection with the arbitration, either from the record of the proceeding or from material or communications related to the arbitration, which the arbitrator has reason to believe may constitute a violation of NASD or FINRA rules, the federal securities laws, or other applicable rules or laws.

Amended by SR-FINRA-2008-021 eff. Dec. 15, 2008.
Adopted by SR-NASD-2003-158 eff. April 16, 2007.

Selected Notices: 07-07, 08-57. 1

12105. Agreement of the Parties

The Customer Code applies to claims filed on or after April 16, 2007. In addition, the list selection provisions of the Customer Code apply to previously filed claims in which a list of arbitrators must be generated after April 16, 2007; in these cases, however, the claim will continue to be governed by the remaining provisions of the old Code unless all parties agree to proceed under the new Code.

a. Except as provided in paragraph (b), if the Code provides that the parties may agree to modify a provision of the Code, or a decision of the Director or the panel, the written agreement of all named parties is required.

b. If the Director or the panel determines that a named party is inactive in the arbitration, or has failed to respond after adequate notice has been given, the Director or the panel may determine that the written agreement of that party is not required while the party is inactive or not responsive. For purposes of this rule, an inactive party could be, but is not limited to: (1) a party that does not answer; (2) a party that answers and then fails to respond to correspondence sent by the Director; (3) a party that answers and then fails to respond to correspondence sent by the panel in cases involving direct communication under Rule 12211; or (4) a party that does not attend pre-hearing conferences.

Amended by SR-FINRA-2008-021 eff. Dec. 15, 2008.
Adopted by SR-NASD-2003-158 eff. April 16, 2007.

Selected Notices: 07-07, 08-57.

PART II
GENERAL ARBITRATION RULES

12200. Arbitration Under an Arbitration Agreement or the Rules of FINRA

The Customer Code applies to claims filed on or after April 16, 2007. In addition, the list selection provisions of the Customer Code apply to previously filed claims in which a list of arbitrators must be generated after April 16, 2007; in these cases, however, the claim will continue to be governed by the remaining provisions of the old Code unless all parties agree to proceed under the new Code.

Parties must arbitrate a dispute under the Code if:

- Arbitration under the Code is either:

  1. Required by a written agreement, or
  2. Requested by the customer;

- The dispute is between a customer and a member or associated person of a member; and
- The dispute arises in connection with the business activities of the member or the associated person, except disputes involving the insurance business activities of a member that is also an insurance company.

Amended by SR-FINRA-2008-021 eff. Dec. 15, 2008.
Adopted by SR-NASD-2003-158 eff. April 16, 2007.

Selected Notices: 07-07, 08-57.

12201. Elective Arbitration

The Customer Code applies to claims filed on or after April 16, 2007. In addition, the list selection provisions of the Customer

Code apply to previously filed claims in which a list of arbitrators must be generated after April 16, 2007; in these cases, however, the claim will continue to be governed by the remaining provisions of the old Code unless all parties agree to proceed under the new Code.

Parties may arbitrate a dispute under the Code if:

- The parties agree in writing to submit the dispute to arbitration under the Code after the dispute arises; and
- The dispute is between a customer and a member, associated person of a member, or other related party; and
- The dispute arises in connection with the business activities of a member or an associated person, except disputes involving the insurance business activities of a member that is also an insurance company.

Amended by SR-FINRA-2008-021 eff. Dec. 15, 2008.
Adopted by SR-NASD-2003-158 eff. April 16, 2007.

Selected Notice: 07-07, 08-57.

12202. Claims Against Inactive Members

The Customer Code applies to claims filed on or after April 16, 2007. In addition, the list selection provisions of the Customer Code apply to previously filed claims in which a list of arbitrators must be generated after April 16, 2007; in these cases, however, the claim will continue to be governed by the remaining provisions of the old Code unless all parties agree to proceed under the new Code.

A claim by or against a member in one of the following categories is ineligible for arbitration under the Code unless the customer agrees in writing to arbitrate after the claim arises:

- A member whose membership is terminated, suspended, cancelled or revoked;
- A member that has been expelled from FINRA; or
- A member that is otherwise defunct.

Amended by SR-FINRA-2008-021 eff. Dec. 15, 2008. Adopted by
SR-NASD-2003-158 eff. April 16, 2007.

Selected Notice: 07-07, 08-57.

12203. Denial of FINRA Forum

**The Customer Code applies to claims filed on or after April 16,
2007. In addition, the list selection provisions of the Customer
Code apply to previously filed claims in which a list of arbitrators
must be generated after April 16, 2007; in these cases, however, the
claim will continue to be governed by the remaining provisions of
the old Code unless all parties agree to proceed under the new Code.**

    a.   The Director may decline to permit the use of the FINRA arbitra-
tion forum if the Director determines that, given the purposes of
FINRA and the intent of the Code, the subject matter of the dispute
is inappropriate, or that accepting the matter would pose a risk to
the health or safety of arbitrators, staff, or parties or their representatives. Only the Director or the President of FINRA Dispute
Resolution may exercise the Director's authority under this rule.

    b.   Disputes that arise out of transactions in a readily identifiable
market may be referred to the arbitration forum for that market, if
the claimant agrees.

Amended by SR-FINRA-2008-021 eff. Dec. 15, 2008.
Adopted by SR-NASD-2003-158 eff. April 16, 2007.

Selected Notices: 07-07, 08-57.

12204. Class Action Claims

**The Customer Code applies to claims filed on or after April 16,
2007. In addition, the list selection provisions of the Customer
Code apply to previously filed claims in which a list of arbitrators
must be generated after April 16, 2007; in these cases, however, the**

claim will continue to be governed by the remaining provisions of the old Code unless all parties agree to proceed under the new Code.

a. Class action claims may not be arbitrated under the Code.
b. Any claim that is based upon the same facts and law, and involves the same defendants as in a court-certified class action or a putative class action, or that is ordered by a court for class-wide arbitration at a forum not sponsored by a self-regulatory organization, shall not be arbitrated under the Code, unless the party bringing the claim files with FINRA one of the following:

   1. a copy of a notice filed with the court in which the class action is pending that the party will not participate in the class action or in any recovery that may result from the class action, or has withdrawn from the class according to any conditions set by the court; or
   2. a notice that the party will not participate in the class action or in any recovery that may result from the class action.

c. The Director will refer to a panel any dispute as to whether a claim is part of a class action, unless a party asks the court hearing the class action to resolve the dispute within 10 days of receiving notice that the Director has decided to refer the dispute to a panel.
d. A member or associated person may not enforce any arbitration agreement against a member of a certified or putative class action with respect to any claim that is the subject of the certified or putative class action until:

   • The class certification is denied;
   • The class is decertified;
   • The member of the certified or putative class is excluded from the class by the court; or
   • The member of the certified or putative class elects not to participate in the class or withdraws from the class according to conditions set by the court, if any.

This paragraph does not otherwise affect the enforceability of any rights under this Code or any other agreement.

Amended by SR-FINRA-2008-021 eff. Dec. 15, 2008.
Adopted by SR-NASD-2003-158 eff. April 16, 2007.
Selected Notice: 07-07, 08-57.

12205. Shareholder Derivative Actions

The Customer Code applies to claims filed on or after April 16, 2007. In addition, the list selection provisions of the Customer Code apply to previously filed claims in which a list of arbitrators must be generated after April 16, 2007; in these cases, however, the claim will continue to be governed by the remaining provisions of the old Code unless all parties agree to proceed under the new Code.

Shareholder derivative actions may not be arbitrated under the Code.

Amended by SR-FINRA-2008-021 eff. Dec. 15, 2008.
Adopted by SR-NASD-2003-158 eff. April 16, 2007.
Selected Notice: 07-07, 08-57.

12206. Time Limits

The Customer Code applies to claims filed on or after April 16, 2007. In addition, the list selection provisions of the Customer Code apply to previously filed claims in which a list of arbitrators must be generated after April 16, 2007; in these cases, however, the claim will continue to be governed by the remaining provisions of the old Code unless all parties agree to proceed under the new Code.

a. **Time Limitation on Submission of Claims**
   No claim shall be eligible for submission to arbitration under the Code where six years have elapsed from the occurrence or event giving rise to the claim. The panel will resolve any questions regarding the eligibility of a claim under this rule.
b. **Dismissal under Rule**

Dismissal of a claim under this rule does not prohibit a party from pursuing the claim in court. By filing a motion to dismiss a claim under this rule, the moving party agrees that if the panel dismisses a claim under this rule, the non-moving party may withdraw any remaining related claims without prejudice and may pursue all of the claims in court.

1. Motions under this rule must be made in writing, and must be filed separately from the answer, and only after the answer is filed.
2. Unless the parties agree or the panel determines otherwise, parties must serve motions under this rule at least 90 days before a scheduled hearing, and parties have 30 days to respond to the motion.
3. Motions under this rule will be decided by the full panel.
4. The panel may not grant a motion under this rule unless an in-person or telephonic prehearing conference on the motion is held or waived by the parties. Prehearing conferences to consider motions under this rule will be recorded as set forth in Rule 12606.
5. If the panel grants a motion under this rule (in whole or part), the decision must be unanimous, and must be accompanied by a written explanation.
6. If the panel denies a motion under this rule, a party may not re-file the denied motion, unless specifically permitted by panel order.
7. If the party moves to dismiss on multiple grounds including eligibility, the panel must decide eligibility first.

   • If the panel grants the motion to dismiss the case on eligibility grounds on all claims, it shall not rule on any other grounds for the motion to dismiss.
   • If the panel grants the motion to dismiss on eligibility grounds on some, but not all claims, and the party against whom the motion was granted elects to move the case to court, the panel shall not rule on any other ground for dismissal for 15 days from the date of service of the panel's decision to grant the motion to dismiss on eligibility grounds.
   • If a panel dismisses any claim on eligibility grounds, the panel

must record the dismissal on eligibility grounds on the face of its order and any subsequent award the panel may issue.

- If the panel denies the motion to dismiss on eligibility grounds, it shall rule on the other bases for the motion to dismiss the remaining claims in accordance with the procedures set forth in Rule 12504(a).

8. If the panel denies a motion under this rule, the panel must assess forum fees associated with hearings on the motion against the moving party.
9. If the panel deems frivolous a motion filed under this rule, the panel must also award reasonable costs and attorneys' fees to any party that opposed the motion.
10. The panel also may issue other sanctions under Rule 12212 if it determines that a party filed a motion under this rule in bad faith.

c. **Effect of Rule on Time Limits for Filing claims in Court**
The rule does not extend applicable statutes of limitations; nor shall the six-year time limit on the submission of claims apply to any claim that is directed to arbitration by a court of competent jurisdiction upon request of a member or associated person. However, when a claimant files a statement of claim in arbitration, any time limits for the filing of the claim in court will be tolled while FINRA retains jurisdiction of the claim.

d. **Effect of Filing a Claim in Court on Time Limits for Filing in Arbitration**
If a party submits a claim to a court of competent jurisdiction, the six-year .time limitation will not run while the court retains jurisdiction of the claim matter.

Amended by SR-FINRA-2009-013 eff. Aug. 10, 2009.
Amended by SR-FINRA-2007-021 eff. Feb. 23, 2009.
Amended by SR-FINRA-2008-021 eff. Dec. 15, 2008.
Amended by SR-NASD-2007-026 eff. April 16, 2007.
Adopted by SR-NASD-2003-158 eff. April 16, 2007.

Selected Notice: 07-07, 08-57, 09-07, 09-36.

12207. Extension of Deadlines

The Customer Code applies to claims filed on or after April 16, 2007. In addition, the list selection provisions of the Customer Code apply to previously filed claims in which a list of arbitrators must be generated after April 16, 2007; in these cases, however, the claim will continue to be governed by the remaining provisions of the old Code unless all parties agree to proceed under the new Code.

a. The parties may agree in writing to extend or modify any deadline for:

- Serving an answer;
- Returning arbitrator or chairperson lists;
- Responding to motions; or Exchanging documents or witness lists.

If the parties agree to extend or modify a deadline under this rule, they must notify the Director of the new deadline in writing.

b. The panel may extend or modify any deadline listed in paragraph (a), or any other deadline set by the panel, either on its own initiative or upon motion of a party.
c. The Director may extend or modify any deadline or time period set by the Code for good cause. The Director may also extend or modify any deadline or time period set by the panel in extraordinary circumstances.

Amended by SR-FINRA-2008-021 eff. Dec. 15, 2008.
Adopted by SR-NASD-2003-158 eff. April 16, 2007.

Selected Notice: 07-07, 08-57.

12208. Representation of Parties

The Customer Code applies to claims filed on or after April 16, 2007. In addition, the list selection provisions of the Customer Code apply to previously filed claims in which a list of arbitrators

must be generated after April 16, 2007; in these cases, however, the claim will continue to be governed by the remaining provisions of the old Code unless all parties agree to proceed under the new Code.

a. **Representation by a Party**

    Parties may represent themselves in an arbitration held in a United States hearing location. A member of a partnership may represent the partnership; and a bona fide officer of a corporation, trust, or association may represent the corporation, trust, or association.

b. **Representation by an Attorney**

    At any stage of an arbitration proceeding held in a United States hearing location, all parties shall have the right to be represented by an attorney at law in good standing and admitted to practice before the Supreme Court of the United States or the highest court of any state of the United States, the District of Columbia, or any commonwealth, territory, or possession of the United States, unless state law prohibits such representation.

c. **Representation by Others**

    Parties may be represented in an arbitration by a person who is not an attorney, unless:

    •   state law prohibits such representation, or
    •   the person is currently suspended or barred from the securities industry in any capacity, or
    •   the person is currently suspended from the practice of law or disbarred.

d. **Qualifications of Representative**

    Issues regarding the qualifications of a person to represent a party in arbitration are governed by applicable law and may be determined by an appropriate court or other regulatory agency. In the absence of a court order, the arbitration proceeding shall not be stayed or otherwise delayed pending resolution of such issues.

Amended by SR-FINRA-2008-021 eff. Dec. 15, 2008.
Amended by SR-NASD-2006-109 eff. Dec. 24, 2007.

Adopted by SR-NASD-2003-158 eff. April 16, 2007.

Selected Notices: 07-07, 07-57, 08-57.

12209. Legal Proceedings

The Customer Code applies to claims filed on or after April 16, 2007. In addition, the list selection provisions of the Customer Code apply to previously filed claims in which a list of arbitrators must be generated after April 16, 2007; in these cases, however, the claim will continue to be governed by the remaining provisions of the old Code unless all parties agree to proceed under the new Code.

During an arbitration, no party may bring any suit, legal action, or proceeding against any other party that concerns or that would resolve any of the matters raised in the arbitration.

Amended by SR-FINRA-2008-021 eff. Dec. 15, 2008.
Adopted by SR-NASD-2003-158 eff. April 16, 2007.

Selected Notice: 07-07, 08-57.

12210. Ex Parte Communications

The Customer Code applies to claims filed on or after April 16, 2007. In addition, the list selection provisions of the Customer Code apply to previously filed claims in which a list of arbitrators must be generated after April 16, 2007; in these cases, however, the claim will continue to be governed by the remaining provisions of the old Code unless all parties agree to proceed under the new Code.

a. Except as provided in Rule 12211, no party, or anyone acting on behalf of a party, may communicate with any arbitrator outside of a scheduled hearing or conference regarding an arbitration unless all parties or their representatives are present.

b. No party, or anyone acting on behalf of a party, may send or give any written motion, request, submission or other materials directly to any

arbitrator, unless the arbitrators and the parties agree, or the Code
provides otherwise.

Amended by SR-FINRA-2008-021 eff. Dec. 15, 2008.
Adopted by SR-NASD-2003-158 eff. April 16, 2007.

Selected Notice: 07-07, 08-57.

12211. Direct Communication Between Parties and Arbitrators

The Customer Code applies to claims filed on or after April 16, 2007. In addition, the list selection provisions of the Customer Code apply to previously filed claims in which a list of arbitrators must be generated after April 16, 2007; in these cases, however, the claim will continue to be governed by the remaining provisions of the old Code unless all parties agree to proceed under the new Code.

(a) This rule provides procedures under which parties and arbitrators may communicate directly.

(b) Only parties that are represented by counsel may use direct communication under this rule. If, during the proceeding, a party chooses to appear *pro se* (without counsel), this rule shall no longer apply.

(c) All arbitrators and all parties must agree to the use of direct communication during the Initial Prehearing Conference or a later conference or hearing before it can be used.

(d) Parties may send the arbitrators only items that are listed in an order.

(e. Parties may send items by regular mail, overnight courier, facsimile, or email. All the arbitrators and parties must have facsimile or email capability before such a delivery method may be used.

(f) Copies of all materials sent to arbitrators must also be sent at the same time and in the same manner to all parties and the Director. Materials that exceed 15 pages, however, shall be sent to the Director only by regular mail or overnight courier.

(g) The Director must receive copies of any orders and decisions made as a result of direct communications among the parties and the arbitrators.

(h) Parties may not communicate orally with any of the arbitrators outside the presence of all parties.

(i)   Any party or arbitrator may terminate the direct communication order at any time, after giving written notice to the other arbitrators and the parties.

Amended by SR-FINRA-2008-021 eff. Dec. 15, 2008.
Adopted by SR-NASD-2003-158 eff. April 16, 2007.

Selected Notice: 07-07, 08-57.

12212. Sanctions

The Customer Code applies to claims filed on or after April 16, 2007. In addition, the list selection provisions of the Customer Code apply to previously filed claims in which a list of arbitrators must be generated after April 16, 2007; in these cases, however, the claim will continue to be governed by the remaining provisions of the old Code unless all parties agree to proceed under the new Code.

a.   The panel may sanction a party for failure to comply with any provision in the Code, or any order of the panel or single arbitrator authorized to act on behalf of the panel.
     Unless prohibited by applicable law, sanctions may include, but are not limited to:

   • Assessing monetary penalties payable to one or more parties; Precluding a party from presenting evidence; Making an adverse inference against a party; Assessing postponement and/or forum fees; and Assessing attorneys' fees, costs and expenses.

b.   The panel may initiate a disciplinary referral at the conclusion of an arbitration.
c.   The panel may dismiss a claim, defense or arbitration with prejudice as a sanction for material and intentional failure to comply with an order of the panel if prior warnings or sanctions have proven ineffective.

Amended by SR-FINRA-2008-021 eff. Dec. 15, 2008.
Adopted by SR-NASD-2003-158 eff. April 16, 2007.

Selected Notice: 07-07, 08-57.

12213. Hearing Locations

The Customer Code applies to claims filed on or after April 16, 2007. In addition, the list selection provisions of the Customer Code apply to previously filed claims in which a list of arbitrators must be generated after April 16, 2007; in these cases, however, the claim will continue to be governed by the remaining provisions of the old Code unless all parties agree to proceed under the new Code.

(a) U.S. Hearing Location

1. The Director will decide which of FINRA's hearing locations will be the hearing location for the arbitration. Generally, the Director will select the hearing location closest to the customer's residence at the time of the events giving rise to the dispute.
2. Before arbitrator lists are sent to the parties under Rule 12403, the parties may agree in writing to a hearing location other than the one selected by the Director.
3. The Director may change the hearing location upon motion of a party, as set forth in Rule 12503.
4. After the panel is appointed, the panel may decide a motion relating to changing the hearing location.

(b) Foreign Hearing Location

(1) If the Director and all parties agree, parties may have their hearing in a foreign hearing location and conducted by foreign arbitrators, provided that the foreign arbitrators have:

A. met FINRA background qualifications for arbitrators;
B. received training on FINRA arbitration rules and procedures; and
C. satisfied at least the same training and testing requirements as those arbitrators who serve in U. S. locations of FINRA.

(2) The parties shall pay an additional surcharge for each day of hearings held in a foreign hearing location. The amount of the surcharge will be determined by the Director and must be agreed to by the parties before the foreign hearing location may be used. This surcharge shall be specified in the agreement to use a foreign hearing location and shall be apportioned equally among the parties, unless they agree otherwise. The foreign arbitrators shall have the authority to apportion this surcharge as provided in Rule 12902(c).

Amended by SR-FINRA-2008-021 eff. Dec. 15, 2008.
Adopted by SR-NASD-2003-158 eff. April 16, 2007.

Selected Notice: 07-07, 08-57.

12214. Payment of Arbitrators

The Customer Code applies to claims filed on or after April 16, 2007. In addition, the list selection provisions of the Customer Code apply to previously filed claims in which a list of arbitrators must be generated after April 16, 2007; in these cases, however, the claim will continue to be governed by the remaining provisions of the old Code unless all parties agree to proceed under the new Code.

(a) Except as provided in paragraph (b) and in Rule 12800, FINRA will pay the panel an honorarium, as follows:

- $200 to each arbitrator for each hearing session in which he or she participates;
- an additional $75 per day to the chairperson for each hearing on the merits;
- $50 for travel to a hearing session that is postponed pursuant to Rule 12601; and
- $100 for each arbitrator if a hearing session other than a prehearing conference is postponed within three business days before a scheduled hearing session pursuant to Rules 12601 (a) (2) and (b) (2) .

(b) The Director may authorize a higher or additional honorarium for the use of a foreign hearing location.

(c) Payment for Deciding Discovery-Related Motions Without a Hearing Session

   (1) FINRA will pay each arbitrator an honorarium of $200 to decide a discoveryrelated motion without a hearing session. This paragraph does not apply to cases administered under Rule 12800.

   (2) For purposes of paragraph (c) (1), a discovery-related motion and any replies or other correspondence relating to the motion shall be considered to be a single motion.

   (3) The panel will allocate the cost of the honoraria under paragraph (c) (1) to the parties pursuant to Rule 12902(c).

(d) Payment for Deciding Contested Subpoena Requests Without a Hearing Session

   1. The honorarium for deciding one or more contested motions requesting the issuance of a subpoena without a hearing session shall be $200. The honorarium shall be paid on a per case basis to each arbitrator who decides the contested motion(s). The parties shall not be assessed more than $600 in fees under this paragraph in any arbitration proceeding. The honorarium shall not be paid for cases administered under Rule 12800.

   2. For purposes of paragraph (d) (1), a contested motion requesting the issuance of a subpoena shall include a motion requesting the issuance of a subpoena, the draft subpoena, a written objection from the party opposing the issuance of the subpoena, and any other documents supporting a party's position.

   3. The panel will allocate the cost of the honorarium under paragraph (d) (1) to the parties pursuant to Rule 12902(c).

(e) Payment for Explained Decisions

   (1) The chairperson who is responsible for writing an explained decision pursuant to Rule 12904(g) will receive an additional honorarium of

$400. The panel will allocate the cost of the honorarium under Rule 12904(g) to the parties.

(2) If the panel decides on its own to write an explained decision, then no panel member will receive the additional honorarium of $400.

Amended by SR-FINRA-2008-051 eff. Apr. 13, 2009.
Amended by SR-FINRA-2008-021 eff. Dec. 15, 2008.
Paragraph (d) Adopted by SR-NASD-2006-101 eff. April 2, 2007.
Paragraphs (a) through (c) adopted by SR-NASD-2003-158 eff. April 16, 2007.

Selected Notice: 07-07, 08-57, 09-16.

PART III
INITIATING AND RESPONDING TO CLAIMS

12300. Filing and Serving Documents

The Customer Code applies to claims filed on or after April 16, 2007. In addition, the list selection provisions of the Customer Code apply to previously filed claims in which a list of arbitrators must be generated after April 16, 2007; in these cases, however, the claim will continue to be governed by the remaining provisions of the old Code unless all parties agree to proceed under the new Code.

(a) Initial statements of claim must be filed with the Director, with enough copies for each other party and each arbitrator. The number of arbitrators is determined in accordance with Rule 12401. The Director will serve the statement of claim on the other parties, and send copies of the statement of claim to each arbitrator.

(b) The parties must serve all other pleadings and other documents directly on each other party. Parties must serve all pleadings on all parties at the same time and in the same manner, unless the parties agree otherwise.

(c) Unless the Code provides otherwise, parties must also file all pleadings and other documents with the Director, with additional copies for each arbitrator. Pleadings and other documents must be filed with the Director at the same time and in the same manner in which they are served on the other parties. Parties filing pleadings and other documents with the Director must include a certificate of service stating the names of the parties served, the date and method of service, and the address (es) to which service was made.

(d) Pleadings and other documents may be filed and served by: first class mail; overnight mail or delivery service; hand delivery; facsimile; or any other method, including electronic mail, that is approved or required by the panel.

(e) Filing and service are accomplished on the date of mailing either by first-class postage prepaid mail or overnight mail service, or, in the case of other means of service, on the date of delivery. Whenever pleadings and other documents must be filed with the Director and served on the other parties, filing and service must occur on the same day and in the same manner, unless the parties agree or the panel directs otherwise.

(f) A party must inform the Director and all other parties in writing of any change of address during an arbitration.

Amended by SR-FINRA-2008-02l eff. Dec. 15, 2008.
Adopted by SR-NASD-2003-l58 eff. April 16, 2007.

Selected Notice: 07-07, 08-57.

12301. Service on Associated Persons

The Customer Code applies to claims filed on or after April 16, 2007. In addition, the list selection provisions of the Customer Code apply to previously filed claims in which a list of arbitrators must be generated after April 16, 2007; in these cases, however, the cla~ will continue to be governed by the remaining provisions of the old Code unless all parties agree to proceed under the new Code.

(a) The Director will serve the initial statement of claim on an associated person directly at the person's residential address or usual place of abode. If service cannot be completed at the person's residential address or usual place of abode, the Director will serve the initial statement of claim on the associated person at the person's business address.

(b) If a member and a person currently associated with the member are named as respondents to the same arbitration, and the Director cannot complete service as provided in paragraph (a), then the Director may serve the member with the initial statement of claim on behalf of the associated person. If service is made on the member, the member must serve the associated person, even if the member will not be representing the associated person in the arbitration. If the member is not representing the associated person in the arbitration, the member must notify, and provide the associated person's current address to, all parties and the Director.

Amended by SR-FINRA-2008-021 eff. Dec. 15, 2008.
Adopted by SR-NASD-2003-158 eff. April 16, 2007.

Selected Notices: 07-07, 08-57.

12302. Filing an Initial Statement of Claim

The Customer Code applies to claims filed on or after April 16, 2007. In addition, the list selection provisions of the Customer Code apply to previously filed claims in which a list of arbitrators must be generated after April 16, 2007; in these cases, however, the claim will continue to be governed by the remaining provisions of the old Code unless all parties agree to proceed under the new Code.

(a) Filing Claim with the Director

    (1) To initiate an arbitration, a claimant must file the following with the Director:

- Signed and dated Submission Agreement; and
- A statement of claim specifying the relevant facts and remedies requested.

    The claimant may include any additional documents supporting the statement of claim.

    (2) A claimant may use the online claim notification and filing procedure to complete part of the arbitration claim filing process through the Internet. To commence this process, a claimant may complete a Claim Information Form that can be accessed through www.finra.org. In completing the Claim Information Form, the claimant may attach an electronic version of the statement of claim, and any additional documents supporting the statement of claim, to the form. Once this online form has been completed, a FINRA Dispute Resolution Tracking Form will be generated and displayed for the claimant to reproduce as necessary. The claimant shall then file with the Director the rest of the materials required in subparagraph (1) of the rule, along with a hard copy of the FINRA Dispute Resolution Tracking Form.

(b) **Number of Copies**

The claimant must file enough copies of the statement of claim, if it has not been submitted electronically, and the signed Submission Agreement, and any additional materials, for the Director, each arbitrator and each other party.

(c) **Fees**

At the time the statement of claim is filed, the claimant must pay all required filing fees.

(d) **Service by Director**

Unless the statement of claim is deficient under Rule 12307, the Director will send a copy of the Submission Agreement, the statement of claim, and any additional materials filed by the claimant, to each other party, and to each arbitrator once the panel has been appointed.

Amended by SR-FINRA-2008-031. eff. Feb. 9, 2009.
Amended by SR-FINRA-2008-021 eff. Dec. 15, 2008.
Amended by SR-FINRA-2007-042 eff. Dec. 27, 2007.
Adopted by SR-NASD-2003-158 eff. April 16, 2007.

Selected Notice: 07-07, 08-57, 09-04.

12303. Answering the Statement of Claim

The Customer Code applies to claims filed on or after April 16, 2007. In addition, the list selection provisions of the Customer Code apply to previously filed claims in which a list of arbitrators must be generated after April 16, 2007; in these cases, however, the claim will continue to be governed by the remaining provisions of the old Code unless all parties agree to proceed under the new Code.

(a) Respondent(s) must directly serve each other party with the following documents within 45 days of receipt of the statement of claim:

- Signed and dated Submission Agreement; and
- An answer specifying the relevant facts and available defenses to the statement of claim.

The respondent may include any additional documents supporting the answer to the statement of claim. Parties that fail to answer in the time provided may be subject to default proceedings under Rule 12801.

(b) The answer to the statement of claim may include any counterclaims against the claimant, cross claims against other respondents, or third party claims, specifying all relevant facts and remedies requested, as well as any additional documents supporting such claim. When serving a third party claim, the respondent must provide each new respondent with copies of all documents previously served by any party, or sent to the parties by the Director.

(c) At the same time that the answer to the statement of claim is served on the other parties, the respondent must file copies of the Submission Agreement, the answer to the statement of claim, and any additional documents, with the Director, with enough copies for the Director and each arbitrator.

d) If the answer to the statement of claim contains any counterclaims, cross claims or third party claims, the respondent must pay all required filing fees.

Amended by SR-FINRA-2008-031. eff. Feb. 9, 2009.
Amended by SR-FINRA-2008-021 eff. Dec. 15, 2008.
Adopted by SR-NASD-2003-158 eff. April 16, 2007.

Selected Notice: 07-07, 08-57, 09-04.

12304. Answering Counterclaims

The Customer Code applies to claims filed on or after April 16, 2007. In addition, the list selection provisions of the Customer Code apply to previously filed claims in which a list of arbitrators must be generated after April 16, 2007; in these cases, however, the claim will continue to be governed by the remaining provisions of the old Code unless all parties agree to proceed under the new Code.

(a) A claimant must directly serve any answer to a counterclaim on each other party within 20 days of receipt of the counterclaim. At the same time, the claimant must file the answer to the counterclaim with the Director with additional copies for each arbitrator.

(b) The answer must include the relevant facts and available defenses to the counterclaim. The claimant may include any additional documents supporting the answer to the counterclaim.

Amended by SR-FINRA-2008-021 eff. Dec. 15, 2008.
Adopted by SR-NASD-2003-158 eff. April 16, 2007.

Selected Notice: 07-07, 08-57.

12305. Answering Cross Claims

The Customer Code applies to claims filed on or after April 16, 2007. In addition, the list selection provisions of the Customer Code apply to previously filed claims in which a list of arbitrators must be generated after April 16, 2007; in these cases, however, the claim will continue to be governed by the remaining provisions of the old Code unless all parties agree to proceed under the new Code.

(a) A respondent must directly serve an answer to a cross claim on each other party within 20 days from the date that the respondent's answer to the statement of claim is due, or from the receipt of the cross claim, whichever is later. At the same time, the respondent must file the answer to the cross claim with the Director with additional copies for each arbitrator.

(b) The answer must include the relevant facts and available defenses to the cross claim. The respondent may include any additional documents supporting the answer to the cross claim.

Amended by SR-FINRA-2008-021 eff. Dec. 15, 2008.
Adopted by SR-NASD-2003-158 eff. April 16, 2007.

Selected Notice: 07-07, 08-57.

12306. Answering Third Party Claims

The Customer Code applies to claims filed on or after April 16, 2007. In addition, the list selection provisions of the Customer Code apply to previously filed claims in which a list of arbitrators must be generated after April 16, 2007; in these cases, however, the claim will continue to be governed by the remaining provisions of the old Code unless all parties agree to proceed under the new Code.

(a) A party responding to a third party claim must directly serve all other parties with the following documents within 45 days of receipt of the third party claim:

   • Signed and dated Submission Agreement; and
   • An answer specifying the relevant facts and available defenses to the third party claim.

   The respondent may include any additional documents supporting the answer to the third party claim.

(b) The answer to the third party claim may also include any counter-claims, cross claims, or third party claims, specifying all relevant facts and remedies requested. The answer may also include any additional documents supporting such claim. When serving a third party claim, the respondent must provide each new respondent with copies of all documents previously served by any party, or sent to the parties by the Director.

(c) At the same time that the answer to the third party claim is served on the other parties, the third party respondent must also file copies of the Submission Agreement, the answer to the third party claim, and any additional documents, with the Director, with additional copies for each arbitrator.

(d) If the answer to the third party claim contains any counterclaim, cross claim or third party claim, the party must also pay all required filing fees.

Amended by SR-FINRA-2008-031. eff. Feb. 9, 2009.
Amended by SR-FINRA-2008-021 eff. Dec. 15, 2008.

Adopted by SR-NASD-2003-158 eff. April 16, 2007.

Selected Notice: 07-07, 08-57, 09-04.

12307. Deficient Claims

The Customer Code applies to claims filed on or after April 16, 2007. In addition, the list selection provisions of the Customer Code apply to previously filed claims in which a list of arbitrators must be generated after April 16, 2007; in these cases, however, the claim will continue to be governed by the remaining provisions of the old Code unless all parties agree to proceed under the new Code.

(a) The Director will not serve any claim that is deficient. The reasons a claim may be deficient include the following:

- A Submission Agreement was not filed by each claimant;
- The Submission Agreement was not properly signed and dated;
- The Submission Agreement does not name all parties named in the claim;
- The claimant did not file the correct number of copies of the Submission Agreement, statement of claim or supporting documents for service on respondents and for the arbitrators;
- The claim does not specify the customer's home address at the time of the events giving rise to the dispute;
- The claim does not specify the claimant's or the claimant's representative's current address; or
- The claimant did not pay all required filing fees, unless the Director deferred the fees.

(b) The Director will notify the claimant in writing if the claim is deficient. If all deficiencies are not corrected within 30 days from the time the claimant receives notice, the Director will close the case without serving the claim, and will refund part of the filing fee in the amount indicated in the schedule under Rule 12900(c).

(c) The panel will not consider any counterclaim, cross claim or third party claim that is deficient. The reasons a counterclaim, cross claim or third party claim may be deficient include the reasons listed in paragraph (a). The Director will notify the party making the counterclaim, cross claim or third party claim of the any deficiencies in writing. If all deficiencies are not corrected within 30 days from the time the party making the counterclaim, cross claim or third party claim receives notice of the deficiency, the panel will proceed with the arbitration as though the deficient counterclaim, cross claim or third party claim had not been made.

Amended by SR-FINRA-2008-031. eff. Feb. 9, 2009.
Amended by SR-FINRA-2009-003 eff. Jan. 8, 2009.
Amended by SR-FINRA-2008-021 eff. Dec. 15, 2008.
Adopted by SR-NASD-2003-158 eff. April 16, 2007.

Selected Notice: 07-07, 08-57, 09-04.

12308. Loss of Defenses Due to Untimely or Incomplete Answer

The Customer Code applies to claims filed on or after April 16, 2007. In addition, the list selection provisions of the Customer Code apply to previously filed claims in which a list of arbitrators must be generated after April 16, 2007; in these cases, however, the claim will continue to be governed by the remaining provisions of the old Code unless all parties agree to proceed under the new Code.

(a) If a party does not answer within the time period specified in the Code, the panel may, upon motion, bar that party from presenting any defenses or facts at the hearing, unless the time to answer was extended in accordance with the Code. The party may also be subject to default proceedings under Rule 12801, if the conditions of Rule 12801(a) apply.

(b) If a party answers a claim that alleges specific facts and contentions with a general denial, or fails to include defenses or relevant facts in its answer that were known to it at the time the answer was filed, the panel may bar that party from presenting the omitted defenses or facts at the hearing.

Amended by SR-FINRA-2008-021 eff. Dec. 15, 2008.
Adopted by SR-NASD-2003-158 eff. April 16, 2007.

Selected Notice: 07-07, 08-57.

12309. Amending Pleadings

The Customer Code applies to claims filed on or after April 16, 2007. In addition, the list selection provisions of the Customer Code apply to previously filed claims in which a list of arbitrators must be generated after April 16, 2007; in these cases, however, the claim will continue to be governed by the remaining provisions of the old Code unless all parties agree to proceed under the new Code.

(a) Before Panel Appointment

Except as provided in paragraph (c), a party may amend a pleading at any time before the panel has been appointed.

(1) To amend a statement of claim that has been filed but not yet served by the Director, the claimant must file the amended claim with the Director, with additional copies for each arbitrator and each other party. The Director will then serve the amended claim in accordance with Rules 12300 and 12301.

(2) To amend any other pleading, a party must serve the amended pleading on each party. At the same time, the party must file the amended pleading with the Director, with additional copies for each arbitrator. If a pleading is amended to add a party to the arbitration, the party amending the pleading must provide each new party with copies of all documents previously served by any party, or sent to the parties by the Director.

(b) After Panel Appointment

Once a panel has been appointed, a party may only amend a pleading if the panel grants a motion to amend in accordance with Rule 12503. Motions to amend a pleading must include a copy of the proposed amended pleading. If the panel grants the motion to amend, the amended pleading does not need to be re-served on the other parties, the Director, or the panel, unless the panel determines otherwise.

(c) **Amendments to Add Parties**

Once the ranked arbitrator lists are due to the Director under Rule 12404(c), no party may amend a pleading to add a new party to the arbitration until a panel has been appointed and the panel grants a motion to add the party. Motions to add a party after panel appointment must be served on all parties, including the party to be added, and the party to be added may respond to the motion in accordance with Rule 12503 without waiving any rights or objections under the Code.

(d) **Responding to an Amended Pleading**

Any party may file a response to an amended pleading, provided the response is filed and served within 20 days of receipt of the amended pleading, unless the panel determines otherwise.

Amended by SR-FINRA-2008-021 eff. Dec. 15, 2008.
Adopted by SR-NASD-2003-158 eff. April 16, 2007.

Selected Notice: 07-07, 08-57.

12310. Answering Amended Claims

The Customer Code applies to claims filed on or after April 16, 2007. In addition, the list selection provisions of the Customer Code apply to previously filed claims in which a list of arbitrators must be generated after April 16, 2007; in these cases, however, the claim will continue to be governed by the remaining provisions of the old Code unless all parties agree to proceed under the new Code.

(a) If a claim is amended before it has been answered, the respondent's original time to answer is extended by 20 days.

(b) If a claim is amended after it has been answered, but before a panel has been appointed, the respondent has 20 days from the time the amended claim is served to serve an amended answer.

(c) If a claim is amended after a panel has been appointed, the respondent has 20 days from the time the respondent receives notice that the panel has granted the motion to amend the claim to serve an amended answer.

(d) The amended answer must be directly served on each other party. At the same time, the amended answer must also be filed with the Director, with additional copies for each arbitrator.

(e) If the amended claim adds a new party to the arbitration, the new party's answer is governed by Rule 12306.

Amended by SR-FINRA-2008-021 eff. Dec. 15, 2008.
Adopted by SR-NASD-2003-158 eff. April 16, 2007.

Selected Notice: 07-07, 08-57.

12311. Amendments to Amount in Dispute

The Customer Code applies to claims filed on or after April 16, 2007. In addition, the list selection provisions of the Customer Code apply to previously filed claims in which a list of arbitrators must be generated after April 16, 2007; in these cases, however, the claim will continue to be governed by the remaining provisions of the old Code unless all parties agree to proceed under the new Code.

If an amended pleading increases the amount in dispute, all filing fees, surcharges and process fees required by the Code will be recalculated based on the new amount in dispute.

Amended by SR-FINRA-2008-021 eff. Dec. 15, 2008.
Adopted by SR-NASD-2003-158 eff. April 16, 2007.

Selected Notice: 07-07, 08-57.

12312. Multiple Claimants

The Customer Code applies to claims filed on or after April 16, 2007. In addition, the list selection provisions of the Customer Code apply to previously filed claims in which a list of arbitrators must be generated after April 16, 2007; in these cases, however, the

claim will continue to be governed by the remaining provisions of the old Code unless all parties agree to proceed under the new Code.

One or more parties may join multiple claims together in the same arbitration if the claims contain common questions of law or fact and: The claims assert any right to relief jointly and severally; or The claims arise out of the same transaction or occurrence, or series of transactions or occurrences. After all responsive pleadings have been served, claims joined together under paragraph (a) of this rule may be separated into two or more arbitrations by the Director before a panel is appointed, or by the panel after the panel is appointed. A party whose claims were separated by the Director may make a motion to the panel in the lowest numbered case to reconsider the director's decision.

Amended by SR-FINRA-2008-021 eff. Dec. 15, 2008.
Adopted by SR-NASD-2003-158 eff. April 16, 2007.

Selected Notice: 07-07, 08-57.

12313. Multiple Respondents

The Customer Code applies to claims filed on or after April 16, 2007. In addition, the list selection provisions of the Customer Code apply to previously filed claims in which a list of arbitrators must be generated after April 16, 2007; in these cases, however, the claim will continue to be governed by the remaining provisions of the old Code unless all parties agree to proceed under the new Code.

(a) One or more parties may name one or more respondents in the same arbitration if the claims contain any questions of law or fact common to all respondents and:

- The claims are asserted against the respondents jointly and severally; or
- The claims arise out of the same transaction or occurrence, or series of transactions or occurrences.

(b) After all responsive pleadings have been served, claims joined together under paragraph (a) of this rule may be separated into two or more arbitrations by the Director before a panel is appointed, or by the panel after the panel is appointed. A party whose claims were separated by the Director may make a motion to the panel in the lowest numbered case to reconsider the Director's decision.

Amended by SR-FINRA-2008-021 eff. Dec. 15, 2008.
Adopted by SR-NASD-2003-158 eff. April 16, 2007.

Selected Notice: 07-07, 08-57.

12314. Combining Claims

The Customer Code applies to claims filed on or after April 16, 2007. In addition, the list selection provisions of the Customer Code apply to previously filed claims in which a list of arbitrators must be generated after April 16, 2007; in these cases, however, the claim will continue to be governed by the remaining provisions of the old Code unless all parties agree to proceed under the new Code.

Before ranked arbitrator lists are due to the Director under Rule 12404(c), the Director may combine separate but related claims into one arbitration. Once a panel has been appointed, the panel may reconsider the Director's decision upon motion of a party.

Amended by SR-FINRA-2008-021 eff. Dec. 15, 2008.
Adopted by SR-NASD-2003-158 eff. April 16, 2007.

Selected Notice: 07-07, 08-57.

PART IV APPOINTMENT, DISQUALIFICATION, AND AUTHORITY OF ARBITRATORS

12400. Neutral List Selection System and Arbitrator Rosters

The Customer Code applies to claims filed on or after April 16, 2007. In addition, the list selection provisions of the Customer Code apply to previously filed claims in which a list of arbitrators must be generated after April 16, 2007; in these cases, however, the claim will continue to be governed by the remaining provisions of the old Code unless all parties agree to proceed under the new Code.

(a) **Neutral List Selection System**

The Neutral List Selection System is a computer system that generates, on a random basis, lists of arbitrators from FINRA's rosters of arbitrators for the selected hearing location for each proceeding. The parties will select their panel through a process of striking and ranking the arbitrators on lists generated by the Neutral List Selection System.

(b) **Arbitrator Rosters**

FINRA maintains the following roster of arbitrators:

A roster of non-public arbitrators as defined in Rule 12100(p);

A roster of public arbitrators as defined in Rule 12100(u); and

A roster of arbitrators who are eligible to serve as chairperson of a panel as described in paragraph (c). Arbitrators who are eligible to serve as chairperson will also be included in the roster of public arbitrators, but will only appear on one list in a case.

(c) **Eligibility for Chairperson Roster**

In customer disputes, chairpersons must be public arbitrators. Arbitrators are eligible for the chairperson roster if they have completed chairperson training provided by FINRA and:

- Have a law degree and are a member of a bar of at least one jurisdiction and have served as an arbitrator through award on at least two arbitrations administered by a self-regulatory organization in which hearings were held; or

- Have served as an arbitrator through award on at least three arbitrations administered by a self-regulatory organization in which hearings were held.

Amended by SR-FINRA-2008-021 eff. Dec. 15, 2008.
Adopted by SR-NASD-2003-158 eff. April 16, 2007.

Selected Notices: 07-07, 08-57.

12401. Number of Arbitrators

The Customer Code applies to claims filed on or after April 16, 2007. In addition, the list selection provisions of the Customer Code apply to previously filed claims in which a list of arbitrators must be generated after April 16, 2007; in these cases, however, the claim will continue to be governed by the remaining provisions of the old Code unless all parties agree to proceed under the new Code.

(a) **Claims of $25,000 or Less**
   If the amount of a claim is $25,000 or less, exclusive of interest and expenses, the panel will consist of one arbitrator and the claim is subject to the simplified arbitration procedures under Rule 12800.

(b) **Claims of More Than $25,000 Up To $100,000**
   If the amount of a claim is more than $25,000 but not more than $100,000, exclusive of interest and expenses, the panel will consist of one arbitrator unless the parties agree in writing to three arbitrators.

(c) **Claims of More Than $100,000; Unspecified or Non-Monetary Claims**
   If the amount of a claim is more than $100,000, exclusive of interest and expenses, or is unspecified, or if the claim does not request money damages, the panel will consist of three arbitrators, unless the parties agree in writing to one arbitrator.

Amended by SR-FINRA-2008-047 eff. March 30, 2009.
Amended by SR-FINRA-2008-021 eff. Dec. 15, 2008.
Adopted by SR-NASD-2003-158 eff. April 16, 2007.

Selected **Notices:** 07-07, 08-57, 09-13.

12402. Composition of Arbitration Panels

The Customer Code applies to claims filed on or after April 16, 2007. In addition, the list selection provisions of the Customer Code apply to previously filed claims in which a list of arbitrators must be generated after April 16, 2007; in these cases, however, the claim will continue to be governed by the remaining provisions of the old Code unless all parties agree to proceed under the new Code.

(a) If the panel consists of one arbitrator, the arbitrator will be a public arbitrator selected from the public chairperson roster, unless the parties agree in writing otherwise.

(b) If the panel consists of three arbitrators, one will be a non-public arbitrator and two will be public arbitrators, one of whom will be selected from the public chairperson roster, unless the parties agree in writing otherwise.

Amended by SR-FINRA-2008-021 eff. Dec. 15, 2008.
Adopted by SR-NASD-2003-158 eff. April 16, 2007.

Selected Notice: 07-07, 08-57.

12403. Generating and Sending Lists to the Parties

The Customer Code applies to claims filed on or after April 16, 2007. In addition, the list selection provisions of the Customer Code apply to previously filed claims in which a list of arbitrators must be generated after April 16, 2007; in these cases, however, the claim will continue to be governed by the remaining provisions of the old Code unless all parties agree to proceed under the new Code.

(a) Generating Lists

(1) If the panel consists of one arbitrator, the Neutral List Selection

System will generate a list of eight public arbitrators from the FINRA chairperson roster.

(2) If the panel consists of three arbitrators, the Neutral List Selection System will generate:

- A list of eight arbitrators from the FINRA non-public arbitrator roster;
- A list of eight arbitrators from the FINRA public arbitrator roster; and
- A list of eight public arbitrators from the FINRA chairperson roster.

(3) If the panel consists of three arbitrators, the Neutral List Selection System will generate the chairperson list first. Chair-qualified arbitrators who were not selected for the chairperson list will be eligible for selection on the public list. An individual arbitrator cannot appear on both the chairperson list and the public list for the same case.

(4) The Neutral List Selection System will exclude arbitrators from the lists based upon current conflicts of interest identified within the Neutral List Selection System.

(b) Sending Lists to Parties

(1) The Director will send the lists generated by the Neutral List Selection System to all parties at the same time, within approximately 30 days after the last answer is due. The parties will also receive employment history for the past 10 years and other background information for each arbitrator listed.

(2) If a party requests additional information about an arbitrator, the Director will request the additional information from the arbitrator, and will send any response to all of the parties at the same time. When a party requests additional information, the Director may, but is not required to, toll the time for parties to return the ranked lists under Rule 12404(c).

Amended by SR-FINRA-2008-021 eff. Dec. 15, 2008.

Adopted by SR-NASD-2003-158 eff. April 16, 2007.

Selected Notice: 07-07, 08-57.

12404. Striking and Ranking Arbitrators

The Customer Code applies to claims filed on or after April 16, 2007. In addition, the list selection provisions of the Customer Code apply to previously filed claims in which a list of arbitrators must be generated after April 16, 2007; in these cases, however, the claim will continue to be governed by the remaining provisions of the old Code unless all parties agree to proceed under the new Code.

(a) Each separately represented party may strike up to four of the arbitrators from each list for any reason by crossing through the names of the arbitrators. At least four names must remain on each list.

(b) Each separately represented party shall rank all remaining arbitrators on the lists in order of preference, with a "1" indicating the party's first choice, a "2" indicating the party's second choice, and so on. Each list of arbitrators must be ranked separately.

(c) The ranked lists must be returned to the Director no more than 20 days after the date upon which the Director sent the lists to the parties. If the Director does not receive a party's ranked lists within that time, the Director will proceed as though the party did not want to strike any arbitrator or have any preferences among the listed arbitrators.

Amended by SR-FINRA-2008-021 eff. Dec. 15, 2008.
Adopted by SR-NASD-2003-158 eff. April 16, 2007.

Selected Notice: 07-07, 08-57.

12405. Combining Lists

The Customer Code applies to claims filed on or after April 16, 2007. In addition, the list selection provisions of the Customer Code apply to previously filed claims in which a list of arbitrators must be generated after April 16, 2007; in these cases, however, the claim

will continue to be governed by the remaining provisions of the old Code unless all parties agree to proceed under the new Code.

For each arbitrator classification (public, non-public, and chairperson), the Director will prepare combined ranked lists of arbitrators based on the parties' numerical rankings, as follows:

- The Director will add the rankings of all claimants together, and the rankings of all respondents together, to produce separate combined ranked lists for the claimants and the respondents.
- The Director will then add the combined rankings of claimants and the respondents together, to produce a single combined ranking number for each arbitrator, excluding all arbitrators stricken by a party.
- The Director will create separate combined ranked lists for each arbitrator classification in cases with both public and non-public arbitrators.

Amended by SR-FINRA-2008-021 eff.Dec.15, 2008.
Adopted by SR-NASD-2003-158 eff. April 16, 2007.

Selected Notice: 07-07, 08-57.

12406. Appointment of Arbitrators; Discretion to Appoint Arbitrators Not on List

The Customer Code applies to claims filed on or after April 16, 2007. In addition, the list selection provisions of the Customer Code apply to previously filed claims in which a list of arbitrators must be generated after April 16, 2007; in these cases, however, the claim will continue to be governed by the remaining provisions of the old Code unless all parties agree to proceed under the new Code.

(a) If the panel consists of one arbitrator, the Director will appoint the highestranked available arbitrator from the combined chairperson list.

(b) If the panel consists of three arbitrators, the Director will appoint:

- The highest-ranked available non-public arbitrator from the combined non-public arbitrator list;
- The highest-ranked available public arbitrator from the combined public arbitrator list, and
- The highest-ranked available public arbitrator from the combined chairperson list, who will serve as chairperson of the panel.

(c) If the number of arbitrators available to serve from the combined list(s) is not sufficient to fill an initial panel, the Director will appoint one or more arbitrators of the required classification to complete the panel from names generated randomly by the Neutral List Selection System. If the Director must appoint a non-public arbitrator, the Director may not appoint a non-public arbitrator as defined in Rule 12100(p) (2) or (3), unless the parties agree otherwise. The Director will provide the parties information about the arbitrators as provided in Rule 12403 and the parties will have the right to challenge the arbitrators as provided in Rule 12410.

(d) Appointment of arbitrators occurs when the Director sends notice to the parties of the names of the arbitrators on the panel. Before making any decision as an arbitrator or attending a hearing session, the arbitrators must execute FINRA's arbitrator oath or affirmation.

Amended by SR-FINRA-2008-021 eff. Dec. 15, 2008.
Adopted by SR-NASD-2003-158 eff. April 16, 2007.

Selected Notice: 07-07, 08-57.

12407. Additional Parties

The Customer Code applies to claims filed on or after April 16, 2007. In addition, the list selection provisions of the Customer Code apply to previously filed claims in which a list of arbitrators must be generated after April 16, 2007; in these cases, however, the claim will continue to be governed by the remaining provisions of the old Code unless all parties agree to proceed under the new Code.

(a) If a party is added to an arbitration after the Director sends the lists generated by the Neutral List Selection System to the parties, but before parties must return the ranked lists to the Director, the Director will send the lists to the newly added party, with employment history for the past 10 years and other background information for each arbitrator listed. The newly added party may rank and strike the arbitrators in accordance with Rule 12404. If the newly added party returns the lists within 20 days after the date upon which the Director sent the lists to the party, the Director will include the new party's lists when combining rankings under Rule 12405. If the Director does not receive the list within that time, the Director will proceed as though the party did not want to strike any arbitrator or have any preference among the listed arbitrators.

(b) Once the ranked lists are due to the Director under Rule 12404, no party may amend a pleading to add a new party to the arbitration until a panel is appointed and grants a motion to add the party. Motions to add a party must be served on all parties, including the party to be added, and the party to be added may respond to the motion in accordance with Rule 12503 without waiving any rights or objections under the Code. If the panel grants the motion to add the party, the newly added party may not strike and rank the arbitrators, but may challenge an arbitrator for cause in accordance with Rule 12410.

Amended by SR-FINRA-2008-021 eff. Dec. 15, 2008.
Adopted by SR-NASD-2003-158 eff. April 16, 2007.

Selected Notice: 07-07, 08-57.

12408. Disclosures Required of Arbitrators

The Customer Code applies to claims filed on or after April 16, 2007. In addition, the list selection provisions of the Customer Code apply to previously filed claims in which a list of arbitrators must be generated after April 16, 2007; in these cases, however, the claim will continue to be governed by the remaining provisions of the old Code unless all parties agree to proceed under the new Code.

(a) Before appointing arbitrators to a panel, the Director will notify the arbitrators of the nature of the dispute and the identity of the parties. Each potential arbitrator must make a reasonable effort to learn of, and must disclose to the Director, any circumstances which might preclude the arbitrator from rendering an objective and impartial determination in the proceeding, including:

(1) Any direct or indirect financial or personal interest in the outcome of the arbitration;

(2) Any existing or past financial, business, professional, family, social, or other relationships or circumstances with any party, any party's representative, or anyone who the arbitrator is told may be a witness in the proceeding, that are likely to affect impartiality or might reasonably create an appearance of partiality or bias;

(3) Any such relationship or circumstances involving members of the arbitrator's family or the arbitrator's current employers, partners, or business associates; and

(4) Any existing or past service as a mediator for any of the parties in the case for which the arbitrator has been selected.

(b) The obligation to disclose interests, relationships, or circumstances that might preclude an arbitrator from rendering an objective and impartial determination described in paragraph (a) is a continuing duty that requires an arbitrator who accepts appointment to an arbitration proceeding to disclose, at any stage of the proceeding, any such interests, relationships, or circumstances that arise, or are recalled or discovered.

(c) The Director will inform the parties to the arbitration of any information disclosed to the Director under this rule unless the arbitrator who disclosed the information declines appointment or voluntarily withdraws from the panel as soon as the arbitrator learns of any interest, relationship or circumstance that might preclude the arbitrator from rendering an objective and impartial determination in the proceeding, or the Director removes the arbitrator.

Amended by SR-FINRA-2008-021 eff. Dec. 15, 2008.
Adopted by SR-NASD-2003-158 eff. April 16, 2007.

Selected Notice: 07-07, 08-57.

12409. Arbitrator Recusal

The Customer Code applies to claims filed on or after April 16, 2007. In addition, the list selection provisions of the Customer Code apply to previously filed claims in which a list of arbitrators must be generated after April 16, 2007; in these cases, however, the claim will continue to be governed by the remaining provisions of the old Code unless all parties agree to proceed under the new Code.

Any party may ask an arbitrator to recuse himself or herself from the panel for good cause. Requests for arbitrator recusal are decided by the arbitrator who is the subject of the request.

Amended by SR-FINRA-2008-021 eff. Dec. 15, 2008.
Adopted by SR-NASD-2003-158 eff. April 16, 2007.

Selected Notice: 07-07, 08-57.

12410. Removal of Arbitrator by Director

The Customer Code applies to claims filed on or after April 16, 2007. In addition, the list selection provisions of the Customer Code apply to previously filed claims in which a list of arbitrators must be generated after April 16, 2007; in these cases, however, the claim will continue to be governed by the remaining provisions of the old Code unless all parties agree to proceed under the new Code.

(a) **Before First Hearing Session Begins**
   Before the first hearing session begins, the Director may remove an arbitrator for conflict of interest or bias, either upon request of a party or on the Director's own initiative.

   (1) The Director will grant a party's request to remove an arbitrator if it is reasonable to infer, based on information known at the time of the request, that the arbitrator is biased, lacks impartiality, or has a direct or indirect interest in the outcome of the arbitration. The interest or bias must be definite and capable of reasonable demonstration, rather

than remote or speculative. Close questions regarding challenges to an arbitrator by a customer under this rule will be resolved in favor of the customer.

(2) The Director must first notify the parties before removing an arbitrator on the Director's own initiative. The Director may not remove the arbitrator if the parties agree in writing to retain the arbitrator within five days of receiving notice of the Director's intent to remove the arbitrator.

(b) After First Hearing Session Begins

After the first hearing session begins, the Director may remove an arbitrator based only on information required to be disclosed under Rule 12408 that was not previously known by the parties. The Director may exercise this authority upon request of a party or on the Director's own initiative. Only the Director or the President of FINRA Dispute Resolution may exercise the Director's authority under this paragraph (b).

Amended by SR-FINRA-2009-003 eff. Jan. 8, 2009.
Amended by SR-FINRA-2008-021 eff. Dec. 15, 2008.
Adopted by SR-NASD-2003-158 eff. April 16, 2007.

Selected Notice: 07-07, 08-57.

12411. Replacement of Arbitrators

The Customer Code applies to claims filed on or after April 16, 2007. In addition, the list selection provisions of the Customer Code apply to previously filed claims in which a list of arbitrators must be generated after April 16, 2007; in these cases, however, the claim will continue to be governed by the remaining provisions of the old Code unless all parties agree to proceed under the new Code.

(a) If an arbitrator is removed, or becomes otherwise unable or unwilling to serve, the Director will appoint a replacement arbitrator in accordance with this rule, unless the parties agree in writing to proceed with only the remaining arbitrators.

(b) The Director will appoint as a replacement arbitrator the arbitrator who is the most highly ranked available arbitrator of the required classification remaining on the combined list.

(c) If there are no available arbitrators of the required classification on the consolidated list, the Director will appoint an arbitrator of the required classification to complete the panel from names generated by the Neutral List Selection System. The Director will provide the parties information about the arbitrator as provided in Rule 12403, and the parties shall have the right to object to the arbitrator as provided in Rule 12410.

(d) If the Director must appoint a non-public arbitrator under paragraph (c), the Director may not appoint a non-public arbitrator as defined in Rule 12100(p) (2) or (3), unless the parties agree otherwise.

Amended by SR-FINRA-2008-021 eff. Dec. 15, 2008.
Adopted by SR-NASD-2003-158 eff. April 16, 2007.

Selected Notice: 07-07, 08-57.

12412. Director's Discretionary Authority

The Customer Code applies to claims filed on or after April 16, 2007. In addition, the list selection provisions of the Customer Code apply to previously filed claims in which a list of arbitrators must be generated after April 16, 2007; in these cases, however, the claim will continue to be governed by the remaining provisions of the old Code unless all parties agree to proceed under the new Code.

The Director may exercise discretionary authority and make any decision that is consistent with the purposes of the Code to facilitate the appointment of arbitrators and the resolution of arbitrations.

Amended by SR-FINRA-2008-021 eff. Dec. 15, 2008.
Adopted by SR-NASD-2003-158 eff. April 16, 2007.

Selected Notice: 07-07, 08-57.

12413. Jurisdiction of Panel and Authority to Interpret the Code

The Customer Code applies to claims filed on or after April 16, 2007. In addition, the list selection provisions of the Customer Code apply to previously filed claims in which a list of arbitrators must be generated after April 16, 2007; in these cases, however, the claim will continue to be governed by the remaining provisions of the old Code unless all parties agree to proceed under the new Code.

The panel has the authority to interpret and determine the applicability of all provisions under the Code. Such interpretations are final and binding upon the parties.

Amended by SR-FINRA-2008-021 eff. Dec. 15, 2008.
Adopted by SR-NASD-2003-158 eff. April 16, 2007.

Selected Notice: 07-07, 08-57.

12414. Determinations of Arbitration Panel

The Customer Code applies to claims filed on or after April 16, 2007. In addition, the list selection provisions of the Customer Code apply to previously filed claims in which a list of arbitrators must be generated after April 16, 2007; in these cases, however, the claim will continue to be governed by the remaining provisions of the old Code unless all parties agree to proceed under the new Code.

All rulings and determinations of the panel must be made by a majority of the arbitrators, unless the parties agree, or the Code or applicable law provides, otherwise.

Amended by SR-FINRA-2008-021 eff. Dec. 15, 2008.
Adopted by SR-NASD-2003-158 eff. April 16, 2007.

Selected Notice: 07-07, 08-57.

PART V
PREHEARING PROCEDURES AND DISCOVERY

12500. Initial Prehearing Conference

The Customer Code applies to claims filed on or after April 16, 2007. In addition, the list selection provisions of the Customer Code apply to previously filed claims *in* which a list of arbitrators must be generated after April 16, 2007; *in* these cases, however, the claim will continue to be governed by the remaining provisions of the old Code unless all parties agree to proceed under the new Code.

(a) After the panel is appointed, the Director will schedule an Initial Prehearing Conference before the panel, except as provided in paragraph (c) of this rule.

(b) The Initial Prehearing Conference will generally be held by telephone. Unless the parties agree otherwise, the Director must notify each party of the time and place of the Initial Prehearing Conference at least 20 days before it takes place.

(c) At the Initial Prehearing Conference, the panel will set discovery, briefing, and motions deadlines, schedule subsequent hearing sessions, and address other preliminary matters. The parties may agree to forgo the Initial Prehearing Conference only if they jointly provide the Director with the following information, in writing, with additional copies for each arbitrator, before the Initial Prehearing Conference is scheduled to be held:

- A statement that the parties accept the panel;
- Whether any other prehearing conferences will be held, and if so, for each prehearing conference, a minimum of four mutually agreeable dates and times, and whether the chairperson or the full panel will preside;
- A minimum of four sets of mutually agreeable hearing dates;
- A discovery schedule;
- A list of all anticipated motions, with filing and response due dates; and

- A determination regarding whether briefs will be submitted, and, if so, the due date for the briefs and any reply briefs.

Amended by SR-FINRA-2008-021 eff. Dec. 15, 2008.
Adopted by SR-NASD-2003-158 eff. April 16, 2007.

Selected Notice: 07-07, 08-57.

12501. Other Prehearing Conferences

The Customer Code applies to claims filed on or after April 16, 2007. In addition, the list selection provisions of the Customer Code apply to previously filed claims *in* which a list of arbitrators must be generated after April 16, 2007; *in* these cases, however, the claim will continue to be governed by the remaining provisions of the old Code unless all parties agree to proceed under the new Code.

(a) A prehearing conference may be scheduled upon the joint request of the parties or at the discretion of the Director. The Director will set the time and place of the prehearing conference and appoint a person to preside.

(b) At a party's request, or at the discretion of the panel, the panel may schedule one or more additional prehearing conferences regarding any outstanding preliminary matters, including:

- Discovery disputes;
- Motions;
- Witness lists and subpoenas;
- Stipulations of fact; Unresolved scheduling issues; Contested issues on which the parties will submit briefs; and Any other matter that will simplify or expedite the arbitration.

(c) The panel will determine the time and place of any additional prehearing conferences. Prehearing conferences will generally be held by telephone. Unless the full panel is required under Rule 12503, prehearing conferences may be held before a single arbitrator, generally the chairperson.

Amended by SR-FINRA-2008-021 eff. Dec. 15, 2008.
Adopted by SR-NASD-2003-158 eff. April 16, 2007.

Selected Notice: 07-07, 08-57.

12502. Recording Prehearing Conferences

The Customer Code applies to claims filed on or after April 16, 2007. In addition, the list selection provisions of the Customer Code apply to previously filed claims in which a list of arbitrators must be generated after April 16, 2007; in these cases, however, the claim will continue to be governed by the remaining provisions of the old Code unless all parties agree to proceed under the new Code.

(a) Prehearing conferences will not be recorded unless the panel determines otherwise, either on its own initiative or upon motion of a party.
(b) If a prehearing conference is recorded, it may be recorded using any of the methods discussed under Rule 12606. The Director will provide a copy of the recording to any party upon request for a nominal fee.

Amended by SR-FINRA-2008-021 eff. Dec. 15, 2008.
Adopted by SR-NASD-2003-158 eff. April 16, 2007.

Selected Notice: 07-07, 08-57.

12503. Motions

The Customer Code applies to claims filed on or after April 16, 2007. In addition, the list selection provisions of the Customer Code apply to previously filed claims in which a list of arbitrators must be generated after April 16, 2007; in these cases, however, the claim will continue to be governed by the remaining provisions of the old Code unless all parties agree to proceed under the new Code.

(a) Motions

(1) A party may make motions in writing, or orally during any hearing session. Before making a motion, a party must make an effort to resolve the matter that is the subject of the motion with the other parties. Every motion, whether written or oral, must include a description of the efforts made by the moving party to resolve the matter before making the motion.

(2 Written motions are not required to be in any particular form, and may take the form of a letter, legal motion, or any other form that the panel decides is acceptable. Written motions must be served directly on each other party, at the same time and in the same manner. Written motions must also be filed with the Director, with additional copies for each arbitrator, at the same time and in the same manner in which they are served on the parties.

(3) Written motions must be served at least 20 days before a scheduled hearing, unless the panel decides otherwise.

(4) Motions to amend a pleading after panel appointment pursuant to Rule 12309(b) must be accompanied by copies of the proposed amended pleading when the motion is served on the other parties and filed with the Director. If the panel grants the motion, the amended pleading does not have to be served again, unless the panel determines otherwise. If a party moves to amend a pleading to add a party, the motion must be served on all parties, including the party to be added, and the party to be added may respond to the motion in accordance with Rule 12309(c) without waiving any rights or objections under the Code.

(b) Responding to Motions

Parties have 10 days from the receipt of a written motion to respond to the motion, unless the moving party agrees to an extension of time, or the Director or the panel decides otherwise. Responses to written motions must be served directly on each other party, at the same time and in the same manner. Responses to written motions must also be filed with the Director, with additional copies for each arbitrator, at the same time and in the same manner in which they are served on the parties.

(c) Authority to Decide Motions

(1) The Director decides motions relating to use of the forum under Rule 12203 and removal of an arbitrator under Rule 12410.

(2) Motions relating to combining or separating claims or arbitrations, or changing the hearing location, are decided by the Director before a panel is appointed, and by the panel after the panel is appointed.

(3) Discovery-related motions are decided by one arbitrator, generally the chairperson. The arbitrator may refer such motions to the full panel either at his or her own initiative, or at the request of a party. The arbitrator must refer motions relating to privilege to the full panel at the request of a party.

(4) Motions for arbitrator recusal under Rule 12409 are decided by the arbitrator who is the subject of the request.

(5) The full panel decides all other motions, including motions relating to the eligibility of a claim under Rule 12206, unless the Code provides or the parties agree otherwise.

Amended by SR-FINRA-2008-021 eff. Dec. 15, 2008.
Adopted by SR-NASD-2003-158 eff. April 16, 2007.

Selected Notice: 07-07, 08-57.

12504. Motions to Dismiss

The Customer Code applies to claims filed on or after April 16, 2007. In addition, the list selection provisions of the Customer Code apply to previously filed claims in which a list of arbitrators must be generated after April 16, 2007; in these cases, however, the claim will continue to be governed by the remaining provisions of the old Code unless all parties agree to proceed under the new Code.

(a) Motions to Dismiss Prior to Conclusion of Case in Chief

(1) Motions to dismiss a claim prior to the conclusion of a party's case in chief are discouraged in arbitration.

(2) Motions under this rule must be made in writing, and must be filed separately from the answer, and only after the answer is filed.

(3) Unless the parties agree or the panel determines otherwise, parties must serve motions under this rule at least 60 days before a scheduled hearing, and parties have 45 days to respond to the motion.

(4) Motions under this rule will be decided by the full panel.

(5) The panel may not grant a motion under this rule unless an in-person or telephonic prehearing conference on the motion is held or waived by the parties. Prehearing conferences to consider motions under this rule will be recorded as set forth in Rule 12606.

(6) The panel cannot act upon a motion to dismiss a party or claim under paragraph (a) of this rule, unless the panel determines that:

    (A) the non-moving party previously released the claim(s) in dispute by a signed settlement agreement and/or written release; or

    (B) the moving party was not associated with the account(s), security(ies), or conduct at issue.

(7) If the panel grants a motion under this rule (in whole or part), the decision must be unanimous, and must be accompanied by a written explanation.

(8) If the panel denies a motion under this rule, the moving party may not re-file the denied motion, unless specifically permitted by panel order.

(9) If the panel denies a motion under this rule, the panel must assess forum fees associated with hearings on the motion against the moving party.

(10)   If the panel deems frivolous a motion filed under this rule, the panel must also award reasonable costs and attorneys' fees to any party that opposed the motion.

(11)   The panel also may issue other sanctions under Rule 12212 if it determines that a party filed a motion under this rule in bad faith.

(b) Motions to Dismiss After Conclusion of Case in Chief

A motion to dismiss made after the conclusion of a party's case in chief is not subject to the procedures set forth in paragraph (a).

(c) Motions to Dismiss Based on Eligibility

A motion to dismiss based on eligibility filed under Rule 12206 will be governed by that rule.

(d) Motions to Dismiss Based on Failure to Comply with Code or Panel Order

A motion to dismiss based on failure to comply with any provision in the Code, or any order of the panel or single arbitrator filed under Rule 12212 will be governed by that rule.

(e) Motions to Dismiss Based on Discovery Abuse

A motion to dismiss based on discovery abuse filed under Rule 12511 will be governed by that rule.

Amended by SR-FINRA-2009-026 eff. Apr. 17, 2009.
Adopted by SR-FINRA-2007-021 eff. Feb. 23, 2009.

Selected Notice: 09-07.

12505. Cooperation of Parties in Discovery

The Customer Code applies to claims filed on or after April 16, 2007. In addition, the list selection provisions of the Customer Code apply to previously filed claims in which a list of arbitrators must be generated after April 16, 2007, in these cases, however, the claim will continue to be governed by the remaining provisions of the old Code unless all parties agree to proceed under the new Code.

The parties must cooperate to the fullest extent practicable in the exchange of documents and information to expedite the arbitration.

Amended by SR-FINRA-200B-021 eff. Dec. 15, 200B.
Adopted by SR-NASD-2003-15B eff. April 16, 2007.

Selected Notice: 07-07, OB-57.

12506. Document Production Lists

The Customer Code applies to claims filed on or after April 16, 2007. In addition, the list selection provisions of the Customer

Code apply to previously filed claims in which a list of arbitrators must be generated after April 16, 2007; in these cases, however, the claim will continue to be governed by the remaining provisions of the old Code unless all parties agree to proceed under the new Code.

(a) **Applicability of Document Production Lists**

When the Director serves the statement of claim, the Director will provide the FINRA Discovery Guide and Document Production Lists to the parties. Document Production Lists 1 and 2 describe the documents that are presumed to be discoverable in all arbitrations between a customer and a member or associated person. Other Document Production Lists may also apply, depending on the specific cause(s) of action alleged.

(b) **Time for Responding to Document Production Lists**

(1) Unless the parties agree otherwise, within 60 days of the date that the answer to the statement of claim is due, or, for parties added by amendment or third party claim, within 60 days of the date that their answer is due, parties must either:

- Produce to all other parties all documents in their possession or control that are described in the Document Production Lists 1 and 2, and any other Document Production List that is applicable based on the cause(s) of action alleged;
- Identify and explain the reason that specific documents described in Document Production Lists 1 and 2, and any other Document Production List that is applicable based on the cause(s) of action alleged, cannot be produced within the required time, and state when the documents will be produced; or
- Object as provided in Rule 12508.

(2) A party must act in good faith when complying with subparagraph (1) of this rule. "Good faith" means that a party must use its best efforts to produce all documents required or agreed to be produced.

If a document cannot be produced in the required time, a party must establish a reasonable timeframe to produce the document.

(c) Redacted Information

For purposes of this rule and Rule 12507, if a party redacts any portion of a document prior to production, the redacted pages (or range of pages) shall be labeled "redacted."

Amended by SR-FINRA-2008-021 eff. Dec. 15, 2008.
Adopted by SR-NASD-2003-158 eff. April 16, 2007.

Selected Notice: 07-07, 08-57.

12507. Other Discovery Requests

The Customer Code applies to claims filed on or after April 16, 2007. In addition, the list selection provisions of the Customer Code apply to previously filed claims in which a list of arbitrators must be generated after April 16, 2007; in these cases, however, the claim will continue to be governed by the remaining provisions of the old Code unless all parties agree to proceed under the new Code.

(a) Making Other Discovery Requests

(1) Parties may also request additional documents or information from any party by serving a written request directly on the party. Requests for information are generally limited to identification of individuals, entities, and time periods related to the dispute; such requests should be reasonable in number and not require narrative answers or fact finding. Standard interrogatories are generally not permitted in arbitration.

(2) Other discovery requests may be served:

- On the claimant, or any respondent named in the initial statement of claim, 45 days or more after the Director serves the statement of claim; and

- On any party subsequently added to the arbitration, 45 days or more after the statement of claim is served on that party.

At the same time, the party must serve copies of the request on all other parties. Any request for documents or information not described in applicable Document Production Lists should be specific, and relate to the matter in controversy.

(b) Responding to Other Discovery Requests

(1) Unless the parties agree otherwise, within 60 days from the date a discovery request other than the Document Production Lists is received, the party receiving the request must either:

- Produce the requested documents or information to all other parties;
- Identify and explain the reason that specific requested documents or information cannot be produced within the required time, and state when the documents will be produced; or
- Object as provided in Rule 12508.

(2) A party must act in good faith when complying with subparagraph (1) of this rule. "Good faith" means that a party must use its best efforts to produce all documents or information required or agreed to be produced. If a document or information cannot be produced in the required time, a party must establish a reasonable timeframe to produce the document or information.

Amended by SR-FINRA-2008-021 eff. Dec. 15, 2008.
Adopted by SR-NASD-2003-158 eff. April 16, 2007.

Selected Notice: 07-07, 08-57.

12508. Objecting to Discovery; Waiver of Objection

The Customer Code applies to claims filed on or after April 16, 2007. In addition, the list selection provisions of the Customer

Code apply to previously filed claims in which a list of arbitrators must be generated after April 16, 2007; in these cases, however, the claim will continue to be governed by the remaining provisions of the old Code unless all parties agree to proceed under the new Code.

(a) If a party objects to producing any document described in Document Production Lists 1 or 2, any other applicable Document Production List, or any document or information requested under Rule 12507, it must specifically identify which document or requested information it is objecting to and why. Objections must be in writing, and must be served on all other parties at the same time and in the same manner. Objections should not be filed with the Director. Parties must produce all applicable listed documents, or other requested documents or information not specified in the objection.

(b) Any objection not made within the required time is waived unless the panel determines that the party had substantial justification for failing to make the objection within the required time.

(c) In making any rulings on objections, arbitrators may consider the relevance of documents or discovery requests and the relevant costs and burdens to parties to produce this information.

Amended by SR-FINRA-2008-021 eff. Dec. 15, 2008.
Adopted by SR-NASD-2003-158 eff. April 16, 2007.

Selected Notice: 07-07, 08-57.

12509. Motions to Compel Discovery

The Customer Code applies to claims filed on or after April 16, 2007. In addition, the list selection provisions of the Customer Code apply to previously filed claims in which a list of arbitrators must be generated after April 16, 2007; in these cases, however, the claim will continue to be governed by the remaining provisions of the old Code unless all parties agree to proceed under the new Code.

(a) A party may make a motion asking the panel to order another party to produce documents or information if the other party has:

- Failed to comply with Rule 12506 or 12507; or
- Objected to the production of documents or information under Rule 12508.

(b) Motions to compel discovery must be made, and will be decided, in accordance with Rule 12503. Such motions must include the disputed document request or list, a copy of any objection thereto, and a description of the efforts of the moving party to resolve the issue before making the motion.

Amended by SR-FINRA-2008-021 eff. Dec. 15, 2008.
Adopted by SR-NASD-2003-158 eff. April 16, 2007.

Selected Notice: 07-07, 08-57.

12510. Depositions

The Customer Code applies to claims filed on or after April 16, 2007. In addition, the list selection provisions of the Customer Code apply to previously filed claims in which a list of arbitrators must be generated after April 16, 2007; in these cases, however, the claim will continue to be governed by the remaining provisions of the old Code unless all parties agree to proceed under the new Code.

Depositions are strongly discouraged in arbitration. Upon motion of a party, the panel may permit depositions, but only under very limited circumstances, including:

- To preserve the testimony of ill or dying witnesses;
- To accommodate essential witnesses who are unable or unwilling to travel long distances for a hearing and may not otherwise be required to participate in the hearing;
- To expedite large or complex cases; and
- If the panel determines that extraordinary circumstances exist.

Amended by SR-FINRA-2008-021 eff. Dec. 15, 2008.
Adopted by SR-NASD-2003-158 eff. April 16, 2007.

Selected Notice: 07-07, 08-57.

12511. Discovery Sanctions

The Customer Code applies to claims filed on or after April 16, 2007. In addition, the list selection provisions of the Customer Code apply to previously filed claims in which a list of arbitrators must be generated after April 16, 2007; in these cases, however, the claim will continue to be governed by the remaining provisions of the old Code unless all parties agree to proceed under the new Code.

Failure to cooperate in the exchange of documents and information as required under the Code may result in sanctions. The panel may issue sanctions against any party in accordance with Rule 12212(a) for:Failing to comply with the discovery provisions of the Code, unless the panel determines that there is substantial justification for the failure to comply; or Frivolously objecting to the production of requested documents or information. (b) The panel may dismiss a claim, defense or proceeding with prejudice in accordance with Rule 12212(c} for intentional and material failure to comply with a discovery order of the panel if prior warnings or sanctions have proven ineffective.

Amended by SR-FINRA-2008-021 eff. Dec. 15, 2008.
Adopted by SR-NASD-2003-158 eff. April 16, 2007.

Selected Notice: 07-07, 08-57.

12512. Subpoenas

The Customer Code applies to claims filed on or after April 16, 2007. In addition, the list selection provisions of the Customer Code apply to previously filed claims in which a list of arbitrators must be generated after April 16, 2007; in these cases, however, the claim will continue to be governed by the remaining provisions of the old Code unless all parties agree to proceed under the new Code.

(a) To the fullest extent possible, parties should produce documents and make witnesses available to each other without the use of subpoenas.

Arbitrators shall have the authority to issue subpoenas for the production of documents or the appearance of witnesses.

(b) A party may make a written motion requesting that an arbitrator issue a subpoena to a party or a non-party. The motion must include a draft subpoena and must be filed with the Director, with an additional copy for the arbitrator. The requesting party must serve the motion and draft subpoena on each other party, at the same time and in the same manner as on the Director. The requesting party may not serve the motion or draft subpoena on a non-party.

(c) If a party receiving a motion and draft subpoena objects to the scope or propriety of the subpoena, that party shall, within 10 calendar days of service of the motion, file written objections with the Director, with an additional copy for the arbitrator, and shall serve copies on all other parties at the same time and in the same manner as on the Director. The party that requested the subpoena may respond to the objections within 10 calendar days of receipt of the objections. After considering all objections, the arbitrator responsible for deciding discovery-related motions shall rule promptly on the issuance and scope of the subpoena.

(d) If the arbitrator issues a subpoena, the party that requested the subpoena must serve the subpoena at the same time and in the same manner on all parties and, if applicable, on any non-party receiving the subpoena.

(e) Any party that receives documents in response to a subpoena served on a non-party shall provide notice to all other parties within five days of receipt of the documents. Thereafter, any party may request copies of such documents and, if such a request is made, the documents must be provided within 10 calendar days following receipt of the request.

Amended by SR-FINRA-2008-021 eff. Dec. 15, 2008.
Adopted by SR-NASD-2003-158 eff. April 2, 2007.

Selected Notices: 07-07, 07-13, 08-57.

12513. Authority of Panel to Direct Appearances of Associated Person Witnesses and Production of Documents Without Subpoenas

The Customer Code applies to claims filed on or after April 16,

2007. In addition, the list selection provisions of the Customer Code apply to previously filed claims in which a list of arbitrators must be generated after April 16, 2007; in these cases, however, the claim will continue to be governed by the remaining provisions of the old Code unless all parties agree to proceed under the new Code.

(a) Upon motion of a party, the panel may order the following without the use of subpoenas: The appearance of any employee or associated person of a member of FINRA; or The production of any documents in the possession or control of such persons or members.

(b) Unless the panel directs otherwise, the party requesting the appearance of witnesses by, or the production of documents from, non-parties under this rule shall pay the reasonable costs of the appearance and/or production.

Amended by SR-FINRA-2008-021 eff. Dec. 15, 2008.
Adopted by SR-NASD-2003-158 eff. April 16, 2007.

Selected Notice: 07-07, 08-57.

12514. Prehearing Exchange of Documents and Witness Lists, and Explained Decision Requests

The Customer Code applies to claims filed on or after April 16, 2007. In addition, the list selection provisions of the Customer Code apply to previously filed claims in which a list of arbitrators must be generated after April 16, 2007; in these cases, however, the claim will continue to be governed by the remaining provisions of the old Code unless all parties agree to proceed under the new Code.

(a) Documents and Other Materials

At least 20 days before the first scheduled hearing date, all parties must provide all other parties with copies of all documents and other materials in their possession or control that they intend to use at the hearing that have not already been produced. The parties should not file the documents with the Director or the arbitrators before the hearing.

(b) Witness Lists

At least 20 days before the first scheduled hearing date, all parties must provide each other party with the names and business affiliations of all witnesses they intend to present at the hearing. At the same time, all parties must file their witness lists with the Director, with enough copies for each arbitrator.

(c) Exclusion of Documents or Witnesses

Parties may not present any documents or other materials not produced and or any witnesses not identified in accordance with this rule at the hearing, unless the panel determines that good cause exists for the failure to produce the document or identify the witness. Good cause includes the need to use documents or call witnesses for rebuttal or impeachment purposes based on developments during the hearing. Documents and lists of witnesses in defense of a claim are not considered rebuttal or impeachment information and, therefore, must be exchanged by the parties.

(d) Explained Decision Request

At least 20 days before the first scheduled hearing date, all parties must submit to the panel any joint request for an explained decision under Rule 12904(g).

Amended by SR-FINRA-2009-026 eff. Apr. 17, 2009.
Amended by SR-FINRA-2008-051 eff. Apr. 13, 2009.
Amended by SR-FINRA-2008-021 eff. Dec. 15, 2008.
Adopted by SR-NASD-2003-158 eff. April 16, 2007.

Selected Notice: 07-07, 08-57, 09-16.

PART VI
HEARINGS; EVIDENCE; CLOSING THE RECORD

12600. Required Hearings

The Customer Code applies to claims filed on or after April 16, 2007. In addition, the list selection provisions of the Customer Code apply to previously filed claims in which a list of arbitrators must be generated after April 16, 2007; in these cases, however, the claim will continue to be governed by the remaining provisions of the old Code unless all parties agree to proceed under the new Code.

(a) Hearings will be held, unless:

- The arbitration is administered under Rule 12800 or Rule 12801;
- The parties agree otherwise in writing; or
- The arbitration has been settled, withdrawn or dismissed.

(b) The panel will decide the time and date of the hearing at the initial prehearing conference or otherwise in another manner.
(c) The Director will notify the parties of the time and place at least 20 days before the hearing begins, unless the parties agree to a shorter time.

Amended by SR-FINRA-2008-021 eff. Dec. 15, 2008.
Adopted by SR-NASD-2003-158 eff. April 16, 2007.

Selected Notice: 07-07, 08-57.

12601. Postponement of Hearings

The Customer Code applies to claims filed on or after April 16, 2007. In addition, the list selection provisions of the Customer Code apply to previously filed claims in which a list of arbitrators must be generated after April 16, 2007; in these cases, however, the

claim will continue to be governed by the remaining provisions of the old Code unless all parties agree to proceed under the new Code.

(a) Postponement of Hearings

(1) When a Hearing Shall Be Postponed
A hearing shall be postponed by agreement of the parties.

(2) When a Hearing May Be Postponed
A hearing may be postponed:

- By the Director, in extraordinary circumstances;
- By the panel, in its own discretion; or
- By the panel, upon motion of a party.

The panel may not grant a motion to postpone a hearing made within 10 days of the date that the hearing is scheduled to begin, unless the panel determines that good cause exists.

(b) Postponement Fees

(1) Except as otherwise provided, a postponement fee will be charged for each postponement agreed to by the parties, or granted upon request of one or more parties. The fee will equal the applicable hearing session fee under Rule 12902. The panel may allocate the fee among the party or parties that agreed to or requested the postponement. The panel may also assess part or all of any postponement fees against a party that did not request the postponement, if the panel determines that the nonrequesting party caused or contributed to the need for the postponement. The panel may waive the fees.

(2) If a postponement request is made by one or more parties and granted within three business days before a scheduled hearing session, the party or parties making the request shall pay an additional fee of $100 per arbitrator. If more than one party requests the postponement, the arbitrators shall allocate the $100 per arbitrator fee among the requesting parties. The arbitrators may allocate all or portion of the $100 per arbitrator fee to the non-requesting party or parties, if the arbitrators determine that the non-requesting party

or parties caused or contributed to the need for the postponement. In the event that a request results in the postponement of consecutively scheduled hearing sessions, the additional fee will be assessed only for the first of the consecutively scheduled hearing sessions. In the event that an extraordinary circumstance prevents a party or parties from making a timely postponement request, arbitrators may use their discretion to waive the fee, provided verification of such circumstance is received.

(3) No postponement fee will be charged if a hearing is postponed: Because the parties agree to submit the matter to mediation at FINRA; By the panel in its own discretion; or By the Director in extraordinary circumstances.

(c) Dismissal of Arbitration Due to Multiple Postponements

If all parties jointly request, or agree to, more than two postponements, the panel may dismiss the arbitration without prejudice.

Amended by SR-FINRA-2008-021 eff. Dec. 15, 2008.
Adopted by SR-NASD-2003-158 eff. April 16, 2007.

Selected Notice: 07-07, 08-57.

12602. Attendance at Hearings

The Customer Code applies to claims filed on or after April 16, 2007. In addition, the list selection provisions of the Customer Code apply to previously filed claims in which a list of arbitrators must be generated after April 16, 2007: in these cases, however, the claim will continue to be governed by the remaining provisions of the old Code unless all parties agree to proceed under the new Code.

The parties and their representatives are entitled to attend all hearings. Absent persuasive reasons to the contrary, expert witnesses should be permitted to attend all hearings. The panel will decide who else may attend any or all of the hearings.

Amended by SR-FINRA-2008-021 eff. Dec. 15, 2008.

Adopted by SR-NASD-2003-158 eff. April 16, 2007.

Selected Notice: 07-07, 08-57.

12603. Failure to Appear

The Customer Code applies to claims filed on or after April 16, 2007. In addition, the list selection provisions of the Customer Code apply to previously filed claims in which a list of arbitrators must be generated after April 16, 2007: in these cases, however, the claim will continue to be governed by the remaining provisions of the old Code unless all parties agree to proceed under the new Code.

If a party fails to appear at a hearing after having been notified of the time, date and place of the hearing, the panel may determine that the hearing may go forward, and may render an award as though all parties had been present.

Amended by SR-FINRA-2008-021 eff. Dec. 15, 2008.
Adopted by SR-NASD-2003-158 eff. April 16, 2007.

Selected Notice: 07-07, 08-57.

12604. Evidence

The Customer Code applies to claims filed on or after April 16, 2007. In addition, the list selection provisions of the Customer Code apply to previously filed claims in which a list of arbitrators must be generated after April 16, 2007: in these cases, however, the claim will continue to be governed by the remaln1ng provisions of the old Code unless all parties agree to proceed under the new Code.

(a) The panel will decide what evidence to admit. The panel is not required to follow state or federal rules of evidence.
(b) Production of documents in discovery does not create a presumption that the documents are admissible at the hearing. A party may state objections to the introduction of any document as evidence at the

hearing to the same extent that any other objection may be raised in arbitration.

Amended by SR-FINRA-2008-021 eff. Dec. 15, 2008.
Adopted by SR-NASD-2003-158 eff. April 16, 2007.

Selected Notice: 07-07, 08-57.

12605. Witness Oath

The Customer Code applies to claims filed on or after April 16, 2007. In addition, the list selection provisions of the Customer Code apply to previously filed claims in which a list of arbitrators must be generated after April 16, 2007; in these cases, however, the claim will continue to be governed by the remaining provisions of the old Code unless all parties agree to proceed under the new Code.

All witnesses must testify under oath or affirmation.

Amended by SR-FINRA-2008-021 eff. Dec. 15, 2008.
Adopted by SR-NASD-2003-158 eff. April 16, 2007.

Selected Notice: 07-07, 08-57.

12606. Record of Proceedings

The Customer Code applies to claims filed on or after April 16, 2007. In addition, the list selection provisions of the Customer Code apply to previously filed claims in which a list of arbitrators must be generated after April 16, 2007; in these cases, however, the claim will continue to be governed by the remaining provisions of the old Code unless all parties agree to proceed under the new Code.

(a) Tape, Digital, or Other Recording

(1) Except as provided in paragraph (b), the Director will make a tape,

digital, or other recording of every hearing. The Director will provide a copy of the recording to any party upon request for a nominal fee.

(2) The panel may order the parties to provide a transcription of the recording. If the panel orders a transcription, copies of the transcription must be provided to each arbitrator and each party. The panel will determine which party or parties must pay the cost of making the transcription and copies.

(3) The recording is the official record of the proceeding, even if it is transcribed.

(b) Stenographic Record

(1) Any party may make a stenographic record of the hearing. Even if a stenographic record is made, the tape, digital, or other recording will be the official record of the proceeding, unless the panel determines otherwise. If the panel determines in advance that the stenographic record will be the official record, the Director will not record the hearing.

(2) If the stenographic record is the official record of the proceeding, a copy must be provided to the Director, each arbitrator, and each other party. The cost of making and copying the stenographic record will be borne by the party electing to make the stenographic record, unless the panel decides that one or more other parties should bear all or part of the costs.

Amended by SR-FINRA-2008-021 eff. Dec. 15, 2008.
Adopted by SR-NASD-2003-158 eff. April 16, 2007.

Selected Notice: 07-07, 08-57.

12607. Order of Presentation of Evidence and Arguments

The Customer Code applies to cla-s filed on or after April 16, 2007. In addition, the list selection provisions of the Customer Code apply to previously filed cla-s in which a list of arbitrators must be generated after April 16, 2007; in these cases, however, the claim

will continue to be governed by the remaining provisions of the old Code unless all parties agree to proceed under the new Code.

Generally, the claimant shall present its case, followed by the respondent's defense. The panel has the discretion to vary the order in which the hearing is conducted, provided that each party is given a fair opportunity to present its case.

Amended by SR-FINRA-2008-021 eff. Dec. 15, 2008.
Adopted by SR-NASD-2003-158 eff. April 16, 2007.

Selected Notice: 07-07, 08-57.

12608. Closing the Record

The Customer Code applies to cla-s filed on or after April 16, 2007. In addition, the list selection provisions of the Customer Code apply to previously filed cla-s in which a list of arbitrators must be generated after April 16, 2007; in these cases, however, the claim will continue to be governed by the remaining provisions of the old Code unless all parties agree to proceed under the new Code.

(a) The panel will decide when the record is closed. Once the record is closed, no further submissions will be accepted from any party.

(b) In cases in which no hearing is held, the record is presumed to be closed when the Director sends the pleadings to the panel, unless the panel requests, or agrees to accept, additional submissions from any party. If so, the record is presumed to be closed when the last such submission is due.

(c) In cases in which a hearing is held, the panel will generally close the record at the end of the last hearing session, unless the panel requests, or agrees to accept, additional submissions from any party. If so, the panel will inform the parties when the submissions are due and when the record will close.

Amended by SR-FINRA-2008-021 eff. Dec. 15, 2008.
Adopted by SR-NASD-2003-158 eff. April 16, 2007.

Selected Notice: 07-07, 08-57.

12609. Reopening the Record

The Customer Code applies to cla~s filed on or after April 16, 2007. In addition, the list selection provisions of the Customer Code apply to previously filed cla~s in which a list of arbitrators must be generated after April 16, 2007; in these cases, however, the claim will continue to be governed by the remaining provisions of the old Code unless all parties agree to proceed under the new Code.

The panel may reopen the record on its own initiative or upon motion of any party at any time before the award is rendered, unless prohibited by applicable law.

Amended by SR-FINRA-2008-021 eff. Dec. 15, 2008.
Adopted by SR-NASD-2003-158 eff. April 16, 2007.

Selected Notice: 07-07, 08-57.

PART VII
TERMINATION OF AN
ARBITRATION BEFORE AWARD

12700. Dismissal of Proceedings Prior to Award

The Customer Code applies to claims filed on or after April 16, 2007. In addition, the list selection provisions of the Customer Code apply to previously filed claims in which a list of arbitrators must be generated after April 16, 2007; in these cases, however, the claim will continue to be governed by the remaining provisions of the old Code unless all parties agree to proceed under the new Code.

(a) The panel must dismiss an arbitration or a claim at the joint request of the parties to that arbitration or claim. The dismissal will be with or without prejudice, depending on the request of the parties.

(b) The panel may dismiss a claim or an arbitration:

- Upon motion of a party under Rule 12206; or
- On its own initiative under Rule 12212(c) or Rule 12601(c).

Amended by SR-FINRA-2008-021 eff. Dec. 15, 2008.
Adopted by SR-NASD-2003-158 eff. April 16, 2007.

Selected Notice: 07-07, 08-57.

12701. Settlement

The Customer Code applies to claims filed on or after April 16, 2007. In addition, the list selection provisions of the Customer Code apply to previously filed claims in which a list of arbitrators must be generated after April 16, 2007; in these cases, however, the claim will continue to be governed by the remaining provisions of the old Code unless all parties agree to proceed under the new Code.

(a) Parties to an arbitration may agree to settle their dispute at any time. Parties who settle must notify the Director. The Director will continue to administer the arbitration, and fees may continue to accrue, until the Director receives written notice of the settlement. The parties do not need to disclose the terms of the settlement agreement to the Director or to FINRA Dispute Resolution, but members and associated persons may have reporting obligations under the rules of FINRA.

(b) Settling parties will remain responsible for fees incurred under the Code. If parties to a settlement fail to agree on the allocation of any outstanding fees, those fees will be divided equally among the settling parties, except member surcharges and prehearing and hearing process fees required by the Code, which will remain the responsibility of the member party or parties.

Amended by SR-FINRA-2008-021 eff. Dec. 15, 2008.
Adopted by SR-NASD-2003-158 eff. April 16, 2007.

Selected Notice: 07-07, 08-57.

12702. Withdrawal of Claims

The Customer Code applies to claims filed on or after April 16, 2007. In addition, the list selection provisions of the Customer Code apply to previously filed claims in which a list of arbitrators must be generated after April 16, 2007; in these cases, however, the claim will continue to be governed by the remaining provisions of the old Code unless all parties agree to proceed under the new Code.

(a) Before a claim has been answered by a party, the claimant may withdraw the claim against that party with or without prejudice.

(b) After a claim has been answered by a party, the claimant may only withdraw it against that party with prejudice unless the panel decides, or the claimant and that party agree, otherwise.

Amended by SR-FINRA-2008-021 eff. Dec. 15, 2008.
Adopted by SR-NASD-2003-158 eff. April 16, 2007.

Selected Notice: 07-07, 08-57.

PART VIII
SIMPLIFIED ARBITRATION
AND DEFAULT PROCEEDINGS

12800. Simplified Arbitration

The Customer Code applies to claims filed on or after April 16, 2007. In addition, the list selection provisions of the Customer Code apply to previously filed claims in which a list of arbitrators must be generated after April 16, 2007; in these cases, however, the claim will continue to be governed by the remaining provisions of the old Code unless all parties agree to proceed under the new Code.

(a) Applicability of Rule

This rule applies to arbitrations involving $25,000 or less, exclusive of interest and expenses. Except as otherwise provided in this rule, all provisions of the Code apply to such arbitrations.

(b) Single Arbitrator

All arbitrations administered under this rule will be decided by a single public arbitrator appointed from the FINRA chairperson roster in accordance with the Neutral List Selection System, unless the parties agree in writing otherwise.

(c) Hearings

(1) No hearing will be held in arbitrations administered under this rule unless the customer requests a hearing.

(2) If no hearing is held, no initial prehearing conference or other prehearing conference will be held, and the arbitrator will render an award based on the pleadings and other materials submitted by the parties. If a hearing is held, the regular provisions of the Code relating to prehearings and hearings, including fee provisions, will apply.

(d) Discovery and Additional Evidence

(1) Document Production Lists, described in Rule 12506, do not apply to arbitrations subject to this rule. However, the arbitrator may, in his or her discretion, choose to use relevant portions of the Document Production Lists in a manner consistent with the expedited nature of simplified proceedings.

(2) The parties may request documents and other information from each other. All requests for the production of documents and other information must be served on all other parties, and filed with the Director, within 30 days from the date that the last answer is due. Any response or objection to a discovery request must be served on all other parties and filed with the Director within 10 days of the receipt of the requests. The arbitrator will resolve any discovery disputes.

(e) Increases in Amount in Dispute

If any pleading increases the amount in dispute to more than $25,000, the arbitration will no longer be administered under this rule, and the regular provisions of the Code will apply. If an arbitrator has been appointed, that arbitrator will remain on the panel. If a three-arbitrator panel is required or requested under Rule 12401, the remaining arbitrators will be appointed by the Director in accordance with Rule 12406(b). If no arbitrator has been appointed, the entire panel will be appointed in accordance with the Neutral List Selection System.

(f) Arbitrator Honoraria

FINRA will pay the arbitrator an honorarium of $125 for each arbitration administered under this rule.

Amended by SR-FINRA-2008-021 eff. Dec. 15, 2008.
Adopted by SR-NASD-2003-158 eff. April 16, 2007.

Selected Notice: 07-07, 08-57.

12801. Default Proceedings

The Customer Code applies to claims filed on or after April 16, 2007. In addition, the list selection provisions of the Customer Code apply to previously filed claims in which a list of arbitrators

must be generated after April 16, 2007; in these cases, however, the claim will continue to be governed by the remaining provisions of the old Code unless all parties agree to proceed under the new Code.

(a) Applicability of Rule

A claimant may request default proceedings against any respondent that falls within one of the following categories and fails to file an answer within the time provided by the Code.

- A member whose membership has been terminated, suspended, canceled, or revoked;
- A member that has been expelled from the FINRA;
- A member that is otherwise defunct; or
- An associated person whose registration is terminated, revoked, or suspended.

(b) Initiating Default Proceedings

(1) To initiate default proceedings against one or more respondents that fail to file a timely answer, the claimant must notify the Director in writing and must send a copy of the notification to all other parties at the same time and in the same manner as the notification was sent to the Director. If there is more than one claimant, all claimants must agree in writing to proceed under this rule against a defaulting respondent before this rule may be used.

(2) If the Director receives written notice from the claimant and determines that the requirements for proceeding under this rule have been met, the Director will:

- Notify all parties that the claim against the defaulting respondent will proceed under this rule; and
- Appoint a single arbitrator in accordance with the Neutral List Selection System to consider the statement of claim and other documents presented by the claimant.

(c) Hearings

No hearing shall be held. The arbitrator may request additional information from the claimant before rendering an award.

(d) Amendments to Increase Relief Requested

Claimants may not amend a claim to increase the relief requested from the defaulting respondent after the Director has notified the parties that the claim will proceed under this rule.

(e) Awards

(1) The arbitrator may not issue an award based solely on the nonappearance of a party. Claimants must present a sufficient basis to support the making of an award. The arbitrator may not award damages in an amount greater than the damages requested in the statement of claim, and may not award any other relief that was not requested in the statement of claim.

(2) The default award shall have no effect on any non-defaulting party.

(f) Respondent's Answer

If a defaulting respondent files an answer after the Director has notified the parties that the claim against that respondent will proceed under this rule but before an award has been issued, the proceedings against that respondent under this rule will be terminated and the claim against that respondent will proceed under the regular provisions in the Code.

Amended by SR-FINRA-2008-021 eff. Dec. 15, 2008.
Adopted by SR-NASD-2003-158 eff. April 16, 2007.

Selected Notice: 07-07, 08-57.

12805. Expungement of Customer Dispute Information under Rule 2080

In order to grant expungement of customer dispute information under Rule 2080, the panel must:

(a) Hold a recorded hearing session (by telephone or in person) regarding the appropriateness of expungement. This paragraph will apply to cases administered under Rule 12800 even if a customer did not request a hearing on the merits.

(b) In cases involving settlements, review settlement documents and consider the amount of payments made to any party and any other terms and conditions of a settlement.

(c) Indicate in the arbitration award which of the Rule 2080 grounds for expungement serve(s) as the basis for its expungement order and provide a brief written explanation of the reason(s) for its finding that one or more Rule 2080 grounds for expungement applies to the facts of the case.

(d) Assess all forum fees for hearing sessions in which the sole topic is the determination of the appropriateness of expungement against the parties requesting expungement relief.

Amended by SR-FINRA-2009-046 eff. Aug. 17, 2009.
Adopted by FINRA-2008-010 and amended by FINRA-2008-063 eff. Dec. 15, 2008.

Selected Notice: 08-79.

PART IX
FEES AND AWARDS

12900. Fees Due When a Claim Is Filed

The Customer Code applies to claims filed on or after April 16, 2007. In addition, the list selection provisions of the Customer Code apply to previously filed claims in which a list of arbitrators must be generated after April 16, 2007; in these cases, however, the claim will continue to be governed by the remaining provisions of the old Code unless all parties agree to proceed under the new Code.

(a) **Fees for Claims Filed by Customers, Associated Persons and Other Non-Members**

   (1) Customers, associated persons, and other non-members who file a claim, counterclaim, cross claim or third party claim must pay a filing fee in the amount indicated in the schedule below. The Director may defer payment of all or part of the filing fee on a showing of financial hardship. If payment of the fee is not deferred, failure to pay the required amount will result in a deficiency under Rule 12307.

   Filing Fees for Claims Filed by Customers, Associated Persons, and Other Non-Members

Amount of Claim (exclusive of interest and expenses)	Filing: Fee
$.01 to $1,000	$50

$1,000.01 to $2,500	$75
$2,500.01 to $5,000	$175
$5,000.01 to $10,000	$325
$10,000.01 to $25,000	$425

$25,000.01 to $50,000	$600
$50,000.01 to $100,000	$975
$100,000.01 to $500,000	$1,425
$500,000.01 to $1 million	$1,575
Over $ 1 million	$1,800
Non-Monetary/Not Specified	$1,250

(2) If the claim does not request or specify money damages, the Director may determine that the filing fee should be more or less than the amount specified in the schedule above, but in any event, the amount of the filing fee may not be less than $50 or more than $1,800.

(b) Fees for Claims Filed by Members

(1) Members filing a claim, counterclaim, cross claim, or third party claim must pay a filing fee in the amount indicated in the schedule below. Failure to pay the required amount will result in a deficiency under Rule 12307.

Fees for Claims Filed by Members

Amount of Claim (exclusive of interest and expanses)	Filing Fee
$.01 to $1,000	$225
$1,000.01 to $2,500	$350
$2,500.01 to $5,000	$525
$5,000.01 to $10,000	$750
$10,000.01 to $25,000	$1,050
$25,000.01 to $50,000	$1,450
$50,000.01 to $100,000	$1,750

$100,000.01 to $500,000	$2,125
$500,000.01 to $1,000,000	$2,450
$1,000,000.01 to $5,000,000	$3,200
Over $5,000,000	$3,700
Non-Monetary/Not Specified	$1,500

   (2) If the claim does not request or specify money damages, the Director may determine that the filing fee should be more or less than the amount specified in the schedule above, but in any event, the filing fee may not be less than $225 or more than $3,700.

(c) Partial Refund of Filing Fee

   (1) If a claim is settled or withdrawn more than 10 days before the date that the hearing on the merits under Rule 12600 is scheduled to begin, a party paying a filing fee will receive a partial refund of the filing fee in the amount indicated in the schedule below, less any other fees or costs assessed against the party under the Code, including any hearing session fees assessed under Rule 12902. No refund will be paid if FINRA receives notice that a claim is settled or withdrawn within 10 days of the date that the hearing on the merits under Rule 12600 is scheduled to begin.

Partial Refund for Settlement or Withdrawal More Than 10 Days Before Hearing on the Merits

Amount of Claim	Refund
(exclusive of interest and expenses)	
$.01 to $1,000	$25
$1,000.01 to $2,500	$50
$2,500.01 to $5,000	$125

$5,000.01 to $10,000	$250
$10,000.01 to $25,000	$300
$25,000.01 to $50,000	$450
$50,000.01 to $100,000	$750
$100,000.01 to $500,000	$1,125
Over $500,000	$1,200
Non-monetary/Not specified	**$1,000**

(2) If the claim does not request or specify money damages, and the Director determines that the hearing session fee should be a different amount than the amount specified in the schedule in Rule 12902, the amount of the refund will be the amount of the hearing session fee determined by the Director, less any fees or costs assessed against the party under the Code, including any hearing session fees assessed under Rule 12902.

(d) Reimbursement of Filing Fees

In the award, the panel may order a party to reimburse another party for all or part of any filing fee paid.

Amended by SR-FINRA-2008-021 eff. Dec. 15, 2008.
Adopted by SR-NASD-2003-158 eff. April 16, 2007.

Selected Notice: 07-07, 08-57.

12901. Member Surcharge

The Customer Code applies to claims filed on or after April 16, 2007. In addition, the list selection provisions of the Customer Code apply to previously filed claims in which a list of arbitrators must be generated after April 16, 2007; in these cases, however, the claim will continue to be governed by the remaining provisions of the old Code unless all parties agree to proceed under the new Code.

(a) Member Surcharge

(1) A surcharge in the amount indicated in the schedule below will be assessed against each member that:

- Files a claim, counterclaim, cross claim, or third party claim under the code;
- Is named as a respondent in a claim, counterclaim, cross claim, or third party claim filed and served under the Code; or
- Employed, at the time the dispute arose, an associated person who is named as a respondent in a claim, counterclaim, cross claim, or third party claim filed and served under the Code. Member Surcharge

Amount in Dispute	Surcharge
	(exclusive of interest and expenses)
Up to $2,500	$150
$2,500.01 to $5,000	$200
$5,000.01 to $10,000	$325
$10,000.01 to $25,000	$425
$25,000.01 to $30,000	$600
$30,000.01 - $50,000	$875
$50,000.01 to $100,000	$1,100
$100,000.01 to $500,000	$1,700
$500,000 to $1,000,000	$2,250
$1,000,000 to $5,000,000	$2,800
$5,000,000 to $10,000,000	$3,350
Over $10,000,000	$3,750
Non-monetary/Not specified	$1,500

(2) If the claim does not request or specify money damages, the Director may determine that the member surcharge should be more or less than the amount specified in the schedule above, but in any event the amount of the member surcharge may not be less than $150 or more than $3,750.

(3) If the claim is filed by the member, the surcharge is due when the claim is filed. If the claim is filed against the member, or against an associated person employed by the member at the time of the events glvlng rise to the dispute, the surcharge is due when the claim is served in accordance with Rule 12300.

(4) No member shall be assessed more than a single surcharge in any arbitration. The panel may not reallocate a surcharge paid by a member to any other party.

(b) Refund of Member Surcharge

(1) The Director will refund the surcharge paid by a member in an arbitration filed by a customer if the panel:

- Denies all of a customer's claims against the member or associated person; and
- Allocates all fees assessed pursuant to Rule 12902(a) against the customer.

(2) The Director may also refund or waive the member surcharge in extraordinary circumstances.

Amended by SR-FINRA-2008-021 eff. Dec. 15, 2008.
Adopted by SR-NASD-2003-158 eff. April 16, 2007.

Selected Notice: 07-07, 08-57.

12902. Hearing Session Fees, and Other Costs and Expenses

The Customer Code applies to claims filed on or after April 16, 2007. In addition, the list selection provisions of the Customer

Code apply to previously filed claims in which a list of arbitrators must be generated after April 16, 2007; in these cases, however, the claim will continue to be governed by the remaining provisions of the old Code unless all parties agree to proceed under the new Code.

(a) Hearing Session Fees

(1) Hearing session fees will be charged for each hearing session. The total amount chargeable to the parties for each hearing session is based on the amount in dispute, as specified in the schedule below. In the award, the panel will determine the amount of each hearing session fee that each party must pay.

Hearing Session Fees

Amount of Claim	Hearing Session w/ One Arbitrator	Hearing Session w/ Three Arbitrators
Up to $2,500	$ 50	N/A
$2,500.01 to $5,000	$ 125	N/A
$5,000.01 to $10,000	$ 250	N/A
$10,000.01 to $25,000	$ 450	N/A
$25,000.01 to $50,000	$ 450	$600
$50,000.01 to $100,000	$ 450	$ 750
$100,000.01 to $500,000	$ 450	$1,125
Over $500,000	$ 450	$1,200
Unspecified Damages	N/A	$1,000

(2) If the claim does not request or specify money damages, the Director may determine that the hearing session fee should be more or less than the amount specified in the schedule above, but in any event the

hearing session fee shall not be less than $50 or more than $1,200 for each hearing session.

(3) If there is more than one claim in a proceeding, the amount of hearing session fees will be based on the largest claim in the proceeding. If any claims are joined or combined under Rules 12312, 12313, or 12314, the amount of those claims will be aggregated and they will be treated as one claim for purposes of this paragraph.

(4) If hearing session fees are allocated against a customer in connection with a claim filed by a member or associated person, the amount of hearing session fees the customer must pay must be based on the amount actually awarded to the member or associated person, rather than on the amount claimed by the member or associated person. No hearing session fees may be assessed against a customer in connection with a claim filed by a member that is dismissed.

(b) Payment of Hearing Session Fees

(1) The panel may assess the hearing session fees in the award, or may require the parties to pay hearing session fees during the course of the arbitration. The total amount that the panel may require the parties to pay for each hearing session during the course of an arbitration may not exceed the total amount chargeable to the parties for each hearing session under the schedule to paragraph (a) of this rule.

(2) Any interim hearing session fee payments made by a party under this rule will be deducted from the total amount of hearing session fees assessed against that party in the award. If the amount of interim payments is more than the amount assessed against the party in the award, the balance will be refunded to that party.

(3) In the award, the amount of one hearing session fee will be deducted from the total amount of hearing session fees assessed against the party who paid the filing fee. If this amount is more than any fees, costs, and expenses assessed against this party under the Code, the balance will be refunded to the party.

(c) Assessment of Other Costs and Expenses in Award

In its award, the panel must also determine the amount of any costs and expenses incurred by the parties under the Code or that are within the scope of the agreement of the parties, and which party or parties will pay those costs and expenses.

(d) Assessment of Hearing Session Fees, Costs, and Expenses in Case of Settlement or Withdrawal

If a claim is settled or withdrawn:

- The parties will be subject to an assessment of hearing session fees for hearing sessions already held.
- If FINRA receives a settlement or withdrawal notice 10 days or fewer prior to the date that the hearing on the merits under Rule 12600 is scheduled to begin, parties that paid a filing fee under Rule 12900 will not be entitled to any refund of the filing fee.
- The parties will also be responsible for any fee or costs incurred under Rules 12502, 12513, 12601, or 12606 in connection with such hearings. If a case is settled or withdrawn and the parties' agreement fails to allocate such fees and costs, the fees and costs will be allocated as provided by Rule 12701(b).

(e) Refund Payments

Any refunds of fees or costs incurred under the Code will be paid directly to the named parties, even if a non-party made a payment on behalf of the named parties.

Amended by SR-FINRA-2008-021 eff. Dec. 15, 2008.
Adopted by SR-NASD-2003-158 eff. April 16, 2007.

Selected Notice: 07-07, 08-57.

12903. Process Fees Paid by Members

The Customer Code applies to claims filed on or after April 16, 2007. In addition, the list selection provisions of the Customer Code apply to previously filed claims in which a list of arbitrators must be generated after April 16, 2007; in these cases, however, the claim will continue to be governed by the remaining provisions of the old Code unless all parties agree to proceed under the new Code.

(a) Each member that is a party to an arbitration in which more than $25,000, exclusive of interest and expenses, is in dispute must pay:

- A non-refundable prehearing process fee of $750, due at the time the parties are sent arbitrator lists in accordance with Rule 12403(b); and
- A non-refundable hearing process fee, due when the parties are notified of the date and location of the hearing on the merits under Rule 12600, as set forth in the schedule below.

Hearing Process Fee Schedule

Amount of Claim (exclusive of interest and expenses)	Hearinsz Process Fee
$1-$25,000	$ 0
$25,000.01-$50,000	$1,000
$50,000.01-$100,000	$1,700
$100,000.01-$500,000	$2,750
$500,000.01-$1,000,000	$4,000
$1,000,000.01-$5,000,000	$5,000
More than $5,000,000	$5,500
Non-Monetary/Not Specified	$2,200

(b) If an associated person of a member is a party, the member that employed the associated person at the time the dispute arose will be charged the process fees, even if the member is not a party. No member shall be assessed more than one prehearing and one hearing process fee in any arbitration.

(c) The panel may not reallocate to any other party any prehearing and hearing process fees paid by a member.

Amended by SR-FINRA-2008-021 eff. Dec. 15, 2008.

Adopted by SR-NASD-2003-158 eff. April 16, 2007.

Selected Notice: 07-07, 08-57.

12904. Awards

The Customer Code applies to claims filed on or after April 16, 2007. In addition, the list selection provisions of the Customer Code apply to previously filed claims in which a list of arbitrators must be generated after April 16, 2007; in these cases, however, the claim will continue to be governed by the remaining provisions of the old Code unless all parties agree to proceed under the new Code.

(a) All awards shall be in writing and signed by a majority of the arbitrators or as required by applicable law. Such awards may be entered as a judgment in any court of competent jurisdiction.

(b) Unless the applicable law directs otherwise, all awards rendered under the Code are final and are not subject to review or appeal.

(c) The Director will serve a copy of the award on each party, or the representative of the party. The Director will serve the award by using any method available and convenient to the parties and the Director, and that is reasonably expected to cause the award to be delivered to all parties, or their representative, on the same day. Methods the Director may use include, but are not limited to, first class, registered or certified mail, hand delivery, and facsimile or other electronic transmission.

(d) The panel shall endeavor to render an award within 30 business days from the date the record is closed.

(e) The award shall contain the following:

- The names of the parties;
- The name of the parties' representatives, if any;
- An acknowledgement by the arbitrators that they have each read the pleadings and other materials filed by the parties;
- A summary of the issues, including the type(s) of any security or product, in controversy;
- The damages and other relief requested;
- The damages and other relief awarded;

- A statement of any other issues resolved;
- The allocation of forum fees and any other fees allocable by the panel;
- The names of the arbitrators;
- The dates the claim was filed and the award rendered;
- The number and dates of hearing sessions;
- The location of the hearings; and
- The signatures of the arbitrators.

(f) The award may contain a rationale underlying the award.

(g) Explained Decisions

(1) This paragraph (g) applies only when all parties jointly request an explained decision.

(2) An explained decision is a fact-based award stating the general reason(s) for the arbitrators' decision. Inclusion of legal authorities and damage calculations is not required.

(3) Parties must make any request for an explained decision no later than the time for the prehearing exchange of documents and witness lists under Rule 12514(d).

(4) The chairperson of the panel will be responsible for writing the explained decision.

(5) The chairperson will receive an additional honorarium of $400 for writing the explained decision, as required by this paragraph (g). The panel will allocate the cost of the chairperson's honorarium to the parties as part of the final award.

(6) This paragraph (g) will not apply to simplified cases decided without a hearing under Rule 12800 or to default cases conducted under Rule 12801.

(h) All awards shall be made publicly available.

(i) Fees and assessments imposed by the arbitrators under the Code shall be paid immediately upon the receipt of the award by the parties. Payment of such fees shall not be deemed ratification of the award by the parties.

(j) All monetary awards shall be paid within 30 days of receipt unless a motion to vacate has been filed with a court of competent jurisdiction. An award shall bear interest from the date of the award:

- If not paid within 30 days of receipt;
- If the award is the subject of a motion to vacate which is denied; or

As specified by the panel in the award.

Interest shall be assessed at the legal rate, if any, then prevailing in the state where the award was rendered, or at a rate set by the arbitrator(s).

Amended by SR-FINRA-2009-026 eff. Apr. 17, 2009.
Amended by SR-FINRA-2008-051 eff. Apr. 13, 2009.
Amended by SR-FINRA-2008-021 eff. Dec. 15, 2008.
Adopted by SR-NASD-2003-158 eff. April 16, 2007.

Selected Notice: 07-07, 08-57, 09-16.

12905. Submissions After a Case Has Closed

The Customer Code applies to claims filed on or after April 16, 2007. In addition, the list selection provisions of the Customer Code apply to previously filed claims in which a list of arbitrators must be generated after April 16, 2007; in these cases, however, the claim will continue to be governed by the rema1n1ng provisions of the old Code unless all parties agree to proceed under the new Code.

(a) Parties may not submit documents to arbitrator(s) in cases that have been closed except under the following limited circumstances:

    (1) as ordered by a court;

    (2) at the request of any party within 10 days of service of an award or notice that a matter has been closed, for typographical or computational errors, or mistakes in the description of any person or property referred to in the award; or

    (3) if all parties agree and submit documents within 10 days of (1) service of an award or (2) notice that a matter has been closed.

(b) Parties must make requests under this rule in writing to the Director and must include the basis relied on under this rule for the request. The Director will forward documents submitted pursuant to paragraph (a) (1), along with any responses from other parties, to the arbitrators. The Director will determine if submissions made pursuant to paragraphs (a) (2) and (a) (3) comply with the grounds enumerated in the rule. If the Director determines that the request complies with paragraphs (a) (2) and (a) (3), the Director will forward the documents, along with any responses from other parties, to the arbitrators. The arbitrators may decline to consider requests that the Director forwards to them under paragraphs (a) (2) and (a) (3) .

(c) Unless the arbitrators rule within 10 days after the Director forwards the documents to the arbitrators pursuant to a request made under paragraphs (a) (2) and (a) (3), the request shall be deemed considered and denied.

(d) Requests under this rule do not extend the time period for payment of any award pursuant to Rule 12904.

Amended by SR-FINRA-2008-057 eff. Dec. 15, 2008.
Adopted by SR-FINRA-2008-005 eff. Nov. 24, 2008

Selected Notice: 08-62

2009 FINRA. All rights reserved. FINRA is a registered trademark of the Financial Industry Regulatory Authority, Inc.
Reprinted with permission from FINRA.

CODE OF MEDIATION PROCEDURE OF THE FINANCIAL INDUSTRY REGULATORY AUTHORITY (FINRA)

2009 FINRA. All rights reserved. FINRA is a registered trademark of the Financial Industry Regulatory Authority, Inc.

Reprinted with permission from FINRA.

14000. CODE OF MEDIATION PROCEDURE

14100. Definitions

Unless otherwise defined in the Code, terms used in the Code and interpretive material, if defined in the FINRA By-Laws, shall have the meaning as defined in the FINRA By-Laws.

(a) **Board**

The term "Board" means the Board of Directors of FINRA Dispute Resolution, Inc.

(b) **Code**

The term "Code" means the Code of Mediation Procedure.

(c) **Director**

The term "Director" in the Rule 14000 Series refers to the Director of Mediation at FINRA Dispute Resolution. Unless the Code or any other FINRA rule provides otherwise, the term includes FINRA staff to whom the Director of Mediation has delegated authority.

(d) **Matter**

The term "matter" means a dispute, claim, or controversy.

(e) **HAMC**

The term "NAMC" means the National Arbitration and Mediation Committee of the Board.

(f) FINRA

Unless the Code specifies otherwise, the term "FINRA" includes FINRA, and FINRA Dispute Resolution, Inc.

(g) FINRA Customer Code

The term "Customer Code" means the Code of Arbitration Procedure for Customer Disputes.

(h) FINRA Industry Code

The term "Industry Code" means the Code of Arbitration Procedure for Industry Disputes.

(i) Submission Agreement

The term "Submission Agreement" means the FINRA Mediation Submission Agreement. The FINRA Mediation Submission Agreement is a document that parties must sign at the outset of a mediation in which they agree to submit to mediation under the Code.

Amended by SR-FINRA-2008-021 eff. Dec. 15, 2008.

Renumbered from Rule 10401 and amended by SR-NASD-2007-022 eff. April 16, 2007.

Adopted by SR-NASD-2004-013 eff. Jan. 30, 2006.

Selected Notices: 05-85, 08-57.

14101. Applicability of Code

The Code applies to any matter submitted to mediation at FINRA.

Amended by SR-FINRA-2008-021 eff. Dec. 15, 2008.

Renumbered from Rule 10402 and amended by SR-NASD-2007-022 eff. April 16, 2007.

Adopted by SR-NASD-2004-013 eff. Jan. 30, 2006.

Selected Notices: 05-85, 08-57.

14102. National Arbitration and Mediation Committee

(a) Pursuant to Section III of the Plan of Allocation and Delegation of Functions by FINRA to Subsidiaries ("Delegation Plan"), the Board shall appoint a National Arbitration and Mediation Committee ("NAMC").

(1) The NAMC shall consist of no fewer than ten and no more than 25 members. At least 50 percent of the NAMC shall be Non-Industry members.

(2) The Chairperson of the Board shall name the Chairperson of the NAMC.

(b) Pursuant to the Delegation Plan, the NAMC shall have the authority to recommend rules, regulations, procedures and amendments relating to arbitration, mediation, and other dispute resolution matters to the Board. All matters recommended by the NAMC to the Board must have been approved by a quorum, which shall consist of a majority of the NAMC, including at least 50 percent of the Non-Industry committee members. If at least 50 percent of the Non-Industry committee members are either (i) present at or (ii) have filed a waiver of attendance for a meeting after receiving an agenda prior to such meeting, the requirement that at least 50 percent of the Non-Industry committee members be present to constitute the quorum shall be waived. The NAMC has such other power and authority as is necessary to carry out the purposes of this Code.

(c) The NAMC may meet as frequently as necessary, but must meet at least once a year.

Amended by SR-FINRA-2008-021 eff. Dec. 15, 2008.
Amended by SR-NASD-2007-026 eff. April 16, 2007.
Renumbered from Rule 104 03 and amended by SR-NASD-2007-022 eff. April 16, 2007.
Adopted by SR-NASD-2004-013 eff. Jan. 30, 2006.

Selected Notices: 05-85, 08-57.

14103. Director of Mediation

(a) The Board shall appoint a Director of Mediation to administer mediations under the Code. The Director will consult with the NAMC on the administration of mediations, as necessary.

(b) The Director may delegate his or her duties when appropriate, unless the Code provides otherwise.

Amended by SR-FINRA-2008-021 eff Dec. 15, 2008.

Renumbered from Rule 104 04 and amended by SR-NASD-2007-022 eff. April 16, 2007.

Adopted by SR-NASD-2004-013 eff. Jan. 30, 2006.

Selected Notices: 05-85, 08-57.

14104. Mediation under the Code

(a) Mediation under the Code is voluntary, and requires the written agreement of all parties. No party may be compelled to participate in a mediation or to settle a matter by FINRA, or by any mediator appointed to mediate a matter pursuant to the Code

(b) If all parties agree, any matter that is eligible for arbitration under the Customer Code or Industry Code, or any part of any such matter, or any dispute related to such matter, including procedural issues, may be submitted for mediation under the Code.

(c) A matter is submitted to mediation when the Director receives an executed Submission Agreement from each party.

(d) The Director shall have the sole authority to determine if a matter is eligible to be submitted for mediation.

Amended by SR-FINRA-2008-021 eff. Dec. 15, 2008.

Renumbered from Rule 10405 and amended by SR-NASD-2007-022 eff. April 16, 2007.

Adopted by SR-NASD-2004-013 eff. Jan. 30, 2006.

Selected Notices: 05-85, 08-57.

14105. Effect of Mediation on Arbitration Proceedings

(a) Unless the parties agree otherwise, the submission of a matter for mediation will not stay or otherwise delay the arbitration of a matter pending at FINRA. If all parties agree to stay an arbitration in order to mediate the matter, the arbitration will be stayed, notwithstanding any provision to the contrary in this Code or any other rule.

(b) If mediation is conducted through FINRA, no postponement fees will be charged for staying the arbitration in order to mediate.

Amended by SR-FINRA-2008-021 eff. Dec. 15, 2008.
Renumbered from Rule 10406 and amended by SR-NASD-2007-022 eff. April 16, 2007.
Adopted by SR-NASD-2004-013 eff. Jan. 30, 2006.

Selected Notices: 05-85, 08-57.

14106. Representation of Parties

(a) Representation by Party
Parties may represent themselves in mediation held in a United States hearing location. A member of a partnership may represent the partnership; and a bona fide officer of a corporation, trust, or association may represent the corporation, trust, or association.

(b) Representation by an Attorney
At any stage of a mediation proceeding held in a United States hearing location, all parties shall have the right to be represented by an attorney at law in good standing and admitted to practice before the Supreme Court of the United States or the highest court of any state of the United States, the District of Columbia, or any commonwealth, territory, or possession of the United States, unless state law prohibits such representation.

(c) Representation by Others
Parties may be represented in mediation by a person who is not an attorney, unless:

- state law prohibits such representation, or
- the person is currently suspended or barred from the securities industry in any capacity, or barred from the securities industry in any capacity, or
- the person is currently suspended from the practice of law or disbarred.

(d) Qualifications of Representatives

Issues regarding the qualifications of a person to represent a party in mediation are governed by applicable law and may be determined by an appropriate court or other regulatory agency. In the absence of a court order, the mediation proceeding shall not be delayed pending resolution of such issues.

Adopted by SR-NASD-2006-109 eff. Dec. 24, 2007.

Selected Notice: 07-57, 08-57.

14107. Mediator Selection

(a) A mediator may be selected:

- By the parties from a list supplied by the Director;
- By the parties from a list or other source of their own choosing; or
- By the Director if the parties do not select a mediator after submitting a matter to mediation.

(b) For any mediator assigned or selected from a list provided by FINRA, the parties will be provided with information relating to the mediator's employment, education, and professional background, as well as information on the mediator's experience, training, and credentials as a mediator.

(c) Any mediator selected or assigned to mediate a matter shall comply with the provisions of Customer Code Rule 12408 or Industry Code Rule 13408, unless, with respect to a mediator selected from a source other than a list provided by FINRA, the parties elect to waive such disclosure.

(d) No mediator may serve as an arbitrator of any matter pending in FINRA arbitration in which he served as a mediator; nor may the mediator represent any party or participant to the mediation in any subsequent FINRA arbitration relating to the subject matter of the mediation.

Amended by SR-FINRA-2008-021 eff. Dec. 15, 2008.

Renumbered from Rule 14106 by SR-NASD-2006-109 eff. Dec. 24 , 2007.
Renumbered from Rule 10407 and amended by SR-NASD-2007-022 eff. April 16, 2007.
Adopted by SR-NASD-2004-013 eff Jan. 30, 2006.

Selected Notices: 05-85, 07-57, 08-57.

14108. Limitation on Liability

FINRA, its employees, and any mediator named to mediate a matter under the Code shall not be liable for any act or omission in connection with a mediation administered under the Code.

Amended by SR-FINRA-2008-021 efJ:. Dec. 15, 2008.
Renumbered from Rule 14107 by SR-NASD-2006-109 eff. Dec. 24 , 2007.
Renumbered from Rule 10408 and amended by SR-NASD-2007-022 eff. April 16, 2007.
Adopted by SR-NASD-2004-013 eff Jan. 30, 2006.

Selected Notices: 05-85, 07-57, 08-57.

14109. Mediation Ground Rules

(a) The following Ground Rules govern the mediation of a matter. The parties to a mediation may agree to amend any or all of the Ground Rules at any time. The Ground Rules are intended to be standards of conduct for the parties and the mediator.

(b) Mediation is voluntary and any party may withdraw from mediation at any time prior to the execution of a written settlement agreement by giving

(c) The mediator shall act as a neutral, impartial, facilitator of the mediation process and shall not have any authority to determine issues, make decisions or otherwise resolve the matter.

(d) Following the selection of a mediator, the mediator, all parties and their representatives will meet in person or by conference call for all mediation sessions, as determined by the mediator or by mutual agreement of the parties. The mediator shall facilitate, through joint sessions, caucuses and/or other means, discussions between the parties, with the goal of assisting the parties in reaching their own resolution of the matter. The mediator shall determine the procedure for the conduct of the mediation. The parties and their representatives agree to cooperate with the mediator in ensuring that the mediation is conducted expeditiously, to make all reasonable efforts to be available for mediation sessions, and to be represented at all scheduled mediation sessions either in person or through a person with authority to settle the matter.

(e) The mediator may meet with and communicate separately with each party or the party's representative. The mediator shall notify all other parties of any such separate meetings or other communications.

(f) The parties agree to attempt, in good faith, to negotiate a settlement of the matter submitted to mediation. Notwithstanding that a matter is being mediated, the parties may engage in direct settlement discussions and negotiations separate from the mediation process.

(g) Mediation is intended to be private and confidential.

(1) The parties and the mediator agree not to disclose, transmit, introduce, or otherwise use opinions, suggestions, proposals, offers, or admissions obtained or disclosed during the mediation by any party or the mediator as evidence in any action at law, or other proceeding, including a lawsuit or arbitration, unless authorized in writing by all other parties to the mediation or compelled by law, except that the fact that a mediation has occurred shall not be considered confidential.

(2) Notwithstanding the foregoing, the parties agree and acknowledge that the provisions of this paragraph shall not operate to shield from disclosure to FINRA or any other regulatory authority, documentary or other information that FINRA or other regulatory authority would be entitled to obtain or examine in the exercise of its regulatory responsibilities.

(3) The mediator will not transmit or otherwise disclose confidential information provided by one party to any other party unless authorized to do so by the party providing the confidential information.

Amended by SR-FINRA-2008-021 eff. Dec. 15, 2008.

Renumbered from Rule 14108 by SR-NASD-2006-109 eff. Dec. 24 , 2007.

Renumbered from Rule 10409 and amended by SR-NASD-2007-022 eff. April 16, 2007.

Adopted by SR-NASD-2004-013 eff Jan. 30, 2006.

Selected Notices: 05-85, 07-57, 08-57.

14110. Mediation Fees

(a) Filing Fees: Cases Filed Directly in Mediation

Each party to a matter submitted directly to a mediation adminis-tered under the Code must pay an administrative fee to FINRA in the amounts indicated in the schedule below, unless such fee is specifically waived by the Director.

Amount in Controversy	Customer and Associated Person Fee	Member Fee
$.01-$25,000	$ 50	$150
$25,000.01-$100,000	$150	$300
Over $100,000	$300	$500

(b) Filing Fees: Cases Initially Filed in Arbitration

When a matter is initially filed in arbitration and subsequently submitted to mediation under the Code, each party must pay an administrative fee to FINRA in the amounts indicated in the schedule below, unless such fee is specifically waived by the Director.

Amount in Controversy	Customer and Associated Person Fee	Member Fee

$.01-$25,000	$ 0	$0
$25,000.01-$100,000	$100	$150
Over $100,000	$250	$500

(c) Mediator Fees and Expenses

The parties to a mediation administered under the Code must pay all of the mediator's charges, including the mediator's travel and other expenses. The charges shall be specified in the Submission Agreement and shall be apportioned equally among the parties unless they agree otherwise. Each party shall deposit with FINRA its proportional share of the anticipated mediator charges and expenses, as determined by the Director, prior to the first mediation session.

Amended by SR-FINRA-2008-021 eff. Dec. 15, 2008.

Renumbered from Rule 14109 by SR-NASD-2006-109 eff. Dec. 24, 2007.

Renumbered from Rule 10410 and amended by SR-NASD-2007-022 eff. April 16, 2007.

Adopted by SR-NASD-2004-013 eff Jan. 30, 2006.

Selected Notices: 05-85, 07-57, 08-57.

© 2009 FINRA. All rights reserved. FINRA is a registered trademark of the Financial Industry Regulatory Authority, Inc.

Reprinted with permission from FINRA.